# A COUNTRY SCANDAL

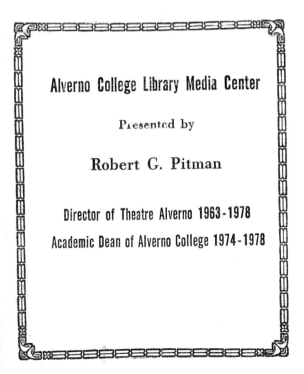

# A COUNTRY SCANDAL

## (Platonov)

## ANTON CHEKHOV

*Translated and Adapted by* ALEX SZOGYI

*COWARD-McCANN, Inc.* New York

© 1960 by Alex Szogyi

Library of Congress Catalog
Number: 61-5693

MANUFACTURED IN THE UNITED STATES OF AMERICA

*For my parents,*
*Ammon, Barbara, and Eliot*

A.S.

# PREFACE

Chekhov's first full-length play has until quite recently been unknown to any large theatregoing public. In the past few years, it has become part of the repertory of two of Europe's finest companies: The Théâtre National Populaire of Avignon and Paris, France, and the Piccolo Teatro of Milan, Italy. This year it entered the repertory of the Vakhtangov Theatre in Moscow, chosen as the play to celebrate the Chekhov centennial in Russia.

Ever since I first discovered the play five years ago, I have wanted to re-create it for an American audience. I felt that it was a fine play, less sophisticated and elusive than the last four great plays of Chekhov, but nevertheless a worthy example of his comic art and one which goes a long way in explaining the origins of his theatrical preoccupations, perhaps even in elucidating his prodigious comic technique. I also wanted to find the way to render Chekhov's succinct, direct language in a modern American idiom which wouldn't falsify (too much) the basic rhythms of the speeches. The major problem posed by this untitled play was that it had to be translated and shaped from a huge manuscript longer than Chekhov's last three plays together. Were it playable, it might have run some six hours. It is Chekhov's earliest extant play, probably his third full-length theatrical effort, written sometime during his twenty-first year, when he was a medical student. After having submitted the manuscript to a well-known actress of the time, Yermolova (at the Maly theatre), who promptly rejected it, Chekhov presumably never again tried to have it performed. He tore up the original; what remains to us now is a long draft with several successive versions indicated in different colored pencils and ink. The speeches of the original manuscript were unwieldy, overstuffed with detail, like fragments from an enormous sketchbook. The play contained some of Chekhov's most irresistible comic writing. What it needed was judicious pruning to retain its silhouette.

The play's title page was destroyed. It was perhaps called *Platonov*, after its hero, a verbose and philosophical Don Juan-in-reverse (another of his early plays, *Ivanov*, was also named for its hero). This gentle and surprisingly elegant farce would be astonishing even if it were not a remarkably coherent play. It contains the largest gallery of characters in all the Chekhov plays. In its prodigious exuberance, it seems almost a pastiche of his later work, for it contains bits and pieces of the later plots and themes, especially *The Cherry Orchard*. It is, however, no pastiche. It simply serves to point up how intact and integral Chekhov's theatrical imagination was at so young an age. It also led me to discover that the translations we have of his plays have often neglected his pungent humor as well as the direct rhythms of his dialogue. It is as if one were to recognize only the sentimentality of Charlie Chaplin's work without any of the comic subtlety. Chekhov's healthy humor had perhaps been stifled in long-winded phrases devoid of the ironic twists of his comic imagination.

Chekhov was a doctor and he began his literary career as a Sunday writer who scribbled for money to support his family. (He called medicine his wife and writing his mistress.) Writing for an audience that readily bought comic vignettes, he chose the farce as his medium in his early theatre, especially in the one-act plays. Yet, despite his labeling his plays as comedies, they have attained the reputation of being ponderous, sad documents of provincial late-nineteenth-century Russia. Chekhov himself was distressed by the false self-pity which was the dominant tone of the Stanislavsky productions. Although Chekhov depicted situations which are ultimately tragic, his characterizations in all the plays are comic in the best Molière and Chaplin tradition.

Although A Country Scandal is not a good old French bedroom farce, it does however capitalize on the surprise entrance and the acceleration of parallel incidents, especially in Act III, when the hero receives many surprise visits. I believe that the play helps to show that Chekhov belongs to the lineage of writers best exemplified by Molière. They both wrote humane and very funny comedies which hold the mirror up to nature, exposing the foibles, deceptions and hypocrisies which epitomize us all. They had the same gift of trenchant wit and scalpel-sharp accuracy of expression.

I have taken a few liberties for the sake of fashioning a coherent play. Chekhov's original ending was interminable; his hero died too slowly, and the other characters lamented too much over him. Every version of the play has in some way modified the ending. I have often reinstated dialogue from Chekhov's first version which seemed fresher than the embroideries of a later version. I have taken one liberty with the plot which no other version has: in order to develop and justify the role of Vengerovich, the usurer, and to make him a more sympathetic and comprehensible individual, I allow him to admit to Anna Petrovna that he wishes to marry her. I have omitted a few characters and a few of the early scenes; Chekhov wrote several characters in pairs where one would easily suffice. I have added some exposition for Sofia, explaining how she met Platonov before the play began. All in all, the liberties I have taken do not exceed those of other versions.

What I have tried to do is to give, in a contemporary idiom, an idea of the delicious comedy inherent in the play. Not only does it provide us with some of Chekhov's richest characterizations, it gives the person interested in Chekhov's development as a dramatist the prototypes and themes of all the later plays. Madame Arkadina and Ranevskaya are spiritual sisters of Anna Petrovna. Triletski gives a hint of Astrov and Dorn. Platonov is another Ivanov and Konstantine. Grekova has moments of Varya. Glagolaev Junior is an incipient Yasha. Only Ossip, the genial horse thief, is unique, and he is one of Chekhov's wildest creations.

A translator-adapter's task is not an easy one. He must revive, resurrect, make live again . . . his is an archeological expedition into words, an experience in an alien language expressing alien concepts in an alien way. Sometimes, ironically enough, in order to capture the spirit of a work, he must violate the strict letter. Nothing is further from a good translation than that misnomer, a literal one. Whatever a translator does, he can never give us the original; what he conjures up in his miraculous hocus-pocus is his conception of what the original was really like. And in the theatre, where a performance depends on a collaboration of many forces, the translator-adapter's work is an endless search for a meaningful language which will make the play live again. The re-creation of a play in the idioms of another language —a blueprint for a special occasion or a particular generation —requires re-translation from decade to decade. Above all, the play must *live*. . . .

[10

# A COUNTRY SCANDAL

# CHARACTERS

ANNA PETROVNA VOINITZEV, widow of General Voinitzev
SERGEY PAVLOVICH VOINITZEV, her stepson
SOFIA EGOROVNA VOINITZEV, his wife

MICHAEL VASSILIEVICH PLATONOV, a schoolteacher
ALEXANDRA IVANOVNA (SACHA) PLATONOV, his young wife
NICHOLAS IVANOVICH TRILETSKI, a doctor, her brother and
    Platonov's friend
IVAN IVANOVICH TRILETSKI, a retired colonel, their father

ABRAM ABRAMOVICH VENGEROVICH, a Jewish merchant
PETRIN, a moneylender
PORFIRY SEMEONOVICH GLAGOLAEV, a rich neighbor of the
    Voinitzev family
KIRYL PORFIRYEVICH GLAGOLAEV, his dissolute son

MARIA EFIMOVA GREKOVA, a young woman scientist
OSSIP, a horse thief

YAKOV and KATYA, servants of Voinitzev
MARKOV, a messenger

> *The action of the play takes place in Voinitzeva,
> a small Russian town, in the 1870s.*

# ACT I

*The scene is a garden in the home of* ANNA
PETROVNA VOINITZEV. *Downstage shrubs and
flowers adorn a winding path. Garden furniture
and lighted lanterns at strategic points. To the
left, we see the façade of a great house. There are
steps leading up to the house. The sound of
laughter and gay conversations is wafted onto the
stage. Bits of music suggest dancing. The house
and garden are both illuminated. The servants,*
YAKOV *and* KATYA, *are hanging lanterns and light-
ing them. It is twilight of a beautiful summer's
day. Visitors walk along the paths of the garden.
Guests and servants descend the terrace and come
into view.*

*(For the sake of clarity, to indicate each essential
beat of the act, we will divide each act into French
scenes; each scene starts with the entrance of a
new character on stage.)*

## SCENE I

*The elder* GLAGOLAEV *comes down the stairs followed by* TRILETSKI, *who is just the slightest bit tipsy.*

TRILETSKI. My dear friend, would you refuse me a small favor? I swear to you before Almighty God, I'm not asking for much.

   GLAGOLAEV *shrugs his shoulders.*

Come come, try to be generous. You have more than you need. Piles and piles. You could buy us all. And more.

   *Pause.*

You're not going to tell me that you don't approve of loans. Well, rest assured, it's not at all a question of a loan . . . I haven't *any* intention of paying you back, I swear it. . . .

GLAGOLAEV. Now *there's* a convincing argument. . . .

TRILETSKI. What a world we live in! The 70s will go down in history as an ungenerous age . . . paralyzed by chronic uncertainty.

   GLAGOLAEV *tries to withdraw.*

Come come, Glagolaev, must I go down on my knees? Where is your heart? You must have a heart somewhere!

GLAGOLAEV (*smiling*). Doctor Triletski, I admire you. As a doctor, you leave much to be desired. But as an extortionist, my compliments.

TRILETSKI. *Touché.*

GLAGOLAEV (*producing his wallet*). Well, how much do you need?

TRILETSKI (*devouring the bills with his eyes*). Holy Mother of God! And they would have us believe that Russia is poor. Where did you get these?

GLAGOLAEV. Here.
> *He gives him the money.*

Fifty rubles. And don't forget; it's the last time.

TRILETSKI. But you're rolling in money. Look, my friend, it's crying out to be spent.
> *Pleading.*

Give it to me.

GLAGOLAEV. Very well, take it. Take it all. If not, you'll steal the shirt off my back. Consider it a down payment. On my health. What a thief you are, Triletski. Professional!

TRILETSKI (*still counting*). Seventy, seventy-five . . .
> *Teasing.*

You're sure they're not counterfeit?

GLAGOLAEV. If that's the way you look at it, give them back.

TRILETSKI (*hiding the bundle quickly*). I would if they were of any use to you. Tell me, Porfiry Semeonovich, why do you lead such an abnormal life? You drink, you argue, you perspire, you stay up all night when you ought to be in bed early. Look at those circles under your eyes, that wan complexion. Really, my friend, you're committing suicide. Tsk, tsk.

GLAGOLAEV. But, Doctor . . .

TRILETSKI. No buts. Don't *doctor* me . . . I don't want to alarm you unduly. You could possibly live several years more. With care. Tell me: are you very rich?

GLAGOLAEV. I could support us both for life. And then some.

TRILETSKI. Then it's really unforgivable. Evenings like this will be the death of you . . . *Entre nous,* do you think I'm blind? I'm on to your tricks. I know why you brave this salon existence.
>*Pause.*

It's the beautiful widow, isn't it?
>*He laughs.*

Really, you'd be better off in bed . . . alone . . .

GLAGOLAEV. Triletski, you go too far. Although you have your amusing moments, you're nothing but a suspicious bastard.
>*He goes into a fit of coughing.*

TRILETSKI. Tsk, tsk. As your doctor and your friend, I prescribe a short rest in the summerhouse. It will do you a world of good.

GLAGOLAEV (*going off*). Perhaps you are right. But you're still a suspicious . . .
>*He leaves.*


# SCENE II

TRILETSKI (*counting his money more carefully*). Banker's money. Peasant's money. How may it best be spent?
>*Servants cross the stage. He gives them each a ruble. They bow and thank him. As they leave,* VOINITZEV *descends the staircase.* ANNA PETROVNA *appears behind him at the window.*

VOINITZEV. But Mama! I've been looking for her everywhere. I don't know where she could be.

[18

ANNA PETROVNA (*sweetly*). Look in the garden, noodle!
> *She goes back into the house.*

VOINITZEV (*calling*). Sofia! Sofia!
> *To* TRILETSKI.

Doctor, I can't find my wife. Have you seen her anywhere?

TRILETSKI. No. I don't think so. But I have something for you. Three adorable rubles.
> *He places the bills in* VOINITZEV's *hand.* VOINITZEV *at first pockets them mechanically, then throws them away angrily and runs into the garden.*

Not even so much as a thank-you. Nauseating. That's present-day humanity for you. No gratitude.
> *He leans over to retrieve the bills.*


## SCENE III

> SACHA *enters, coming from the house, pushing her father ahead of her.*

SACHA. Let's please go now.

IVAN TRILETSKI. But why, my dear?

SACHA. It's not yet dinnertime and already you're hopelessly drunk. Aren't you ashamed to humiliate me in this way?

IVAN TRILETSKI. My child, you're so naïve! You could never understand a man like myself. Your mother was the same. Same hair, same eyes, same sweet little goose. God rest her soul.

SACHA. Father!

IVAN TRILETSKI. I'm not the only one. Look at that dignified creature . . .

*Indicating his son,* NICHOLAS.
sprawled on the lawn.

SACHA. My God, will it never stop? Get up, Nicholas. Isn't it enough your father drinks? Not you, too . . .

NICHOLAS TRILETSKI. Patience. Patience. I'm putting a little money aside.

SACHA. Nicholas, don't you ever consider your position? A doctor ought to be an example . . .

IVAN TRILETSKI. She's right. Absolutely right!

SACHA. And Father, at your age. You really must care more what people think of you . . . Shame . . .

IVAN TRILETSKI. Sacha, my little flower. You're delirious. I cannot lie. I have tippled. And why not? I'm a military man. In the army, one understands these things. That's life. . . . If I had stayed in the army a little longer, I would now be a general. Think of it.

SACHA. Come home.

IVAN TRILETSKI. I said, a general.

SACHA. Generals do not drink. Come.

IVAN TRILETSKI. What are you saying? Generals are made of drink. In the army we have *joie de vivre*. My child, you're just like your poor mother. She spent her entire life criticizing the inevitable. Neither of you ever understood me. When I think I'll never see her sweet face again . . . Oh, how I loved her. God gave her to me, and God took her away.
*Kneeling.*
Forgive me, Sacha. I'm an old fool, but you're my daughter. Tell me you forgive me.

SACHA. Of course, I forgive you. I forgive you. Get up.

IVAN TRILETSKI. Swear you forgive me.

SACHA. I swear it. But you'll promise me something, too.

IVAN TRILETSKI. And that is . . .

SACHA. Promise me you'll give up drinking. If Nicholas conducts himself shamelessly, well and good! But that behavior is unworthy of an elderly gentleman, such as yourself.

IVAN TRILETSKI. My little one, the shadow of your dear departed mother lives on in you. From this moment, not a drop of alcohol will cross these lips. On my honor, as a soldier. However, if it's prescribed as medicine . . .

SACHA. I think Michael is in the summerhouse. I'll tell him we're leaving.
*She exits to summerhouse.*

NICHOLAS TRILETSKI (*he has picked up the bills and approaches his father*). One hundred kopecks, Father. For your medication.

IVAN TRILETSKI. One hundred kopecks? Young man, are you by any chance the son of Colonel Ivan Ivanovich Triletski, who served in the Imperial Guard?

NICHOLAS TRILETSKI. I am.

IVAN TRILETSKI. In that case, I receive it willingly.
*They both laugh.*
Thank you. I refuse charity, but I accept a son's gift. I am honest. Yet, in my life I have witnessed such utter corruption it could be called . . . Babylonian. I was above it all.

NICHOLAS TRILETSKI. Father, we owe it to ourselves to be modest.

IVAN TRILETSKI. I am modest. I was simply giving you a sermon. Will I not have to answer for you before God? Good night.

NICHOLAS TRILETSKI. Where are you going?

IVAN TRILETSKI. Home. Sacha, poor dear, must be taken home. Evening parties frighten her. It's unfortunate to see people behaving as they actually are. I'll put her to bed and I'll be right back.

NICHOLAS TRILETSKI. Here, take three rubles for the trip.

IVAN TRILETSKI (*suddenly angry*). Did I not make myself understood? There hasn't been the slightest taint of corruption in *my* life. My son, when I served during the war against the Turks . . .

NICHOLAS TRILETSKI. Bravo, Colonel! Forward march . . . one-two, one-two . . .

SACHA (*returns*). Let's go. Please . . .

IVAN TRILETSKI. May God protect you, Nicholas. You are a good man. Your brother-in-law Michael Platonov is a freethinker but he too, God rest his soul, is a good man. And Anna Petrovna . . .
      SACHA *drags him off stage.*
I'm coming. I'm coming. One-two, one-two.

SACHA. You're nothing but a child.

IVAN TRILETSKI. Yes, it's true. Aren't we all? One-two, one-two . . .

## SCENE IV

PETRIN *and* VENGEROVICH, *usurers, enter arm in arm.*

PETRIN. Well, Abram Abramovich, you may put fifty thousand rubles right here, in front of me, and I swear, I'll steal them. But I don't intend to be caught. Anyone would do the same. You, too. Don't try to deny it.

VENGEROVICH. No. Not me.

PETRIN. I'd steal even one measly ruble. Honesty, ugh! An honest man is stupid.

VENGEROVICH. Then I am stupid, Petrin.

NICHOLAS TRILETSKI. Here's a ruble for your honesty, my friends.
*He gives each of them a bill.*

VENGEROVICH (*as they pocket them*). Oh, thank you, Doctor.

PETRIN. Well, that disappeared like lightning, honest Vengerovich.
ANNA PETROVNA *appears at the window.*

ANNA PETROVNA. Triletski, give me a ruble too, eh?
*She disappears from the window.*

NICHOLAS TRILETSKI. No, not one, but five, since you are a major general's wife. And I'll bring it to you . . . personally.
*He enters the house.*

## SCENE V

PETRIN. I can't stand that woman. Proud creature. She's too showy. Widows ought at least to be discreet and quiet. They've nothing to boast about.

VENGEROVICH. Still, Glagolaev is fond of her.

PETRIN. He's senile, money or no money.

VENGEROVICH. He chases her at every party. Sits there, gaping, like an idiot, until she looks back at him. I ask you, is that how to woo a woman?

PETRIN. They say he wants to marry her.

VENGEROVICH. At his age!
        *He sneers.*
He's a hundred years old if he's a day.

PETRIN. That may be, but I'd like to see them married. Since her husband's death, the widow has swallowed up all the family money. And what she hasn't swallowed up, her stepson has. As you well know, the house and property are mortgaged.
        *Pause.*
If she married old Glagolaev, I might get my money back. I'd sell my shares of the mortgage. She owes me sixteen thousand rubles. Think of it.

VENGEROVICH (*as they go off*). And she owes me more than that. . . .
        *They disappear into the house.*

## SCENE VI

SOFIA *and* VOINITZEV *enter; they speak quickly, as if they have been quarreling.*

SOFIA. I have nothing more to say to you.

VOINITZEV. It's too soon to have secrets from your husband.
*They sit down on a bench.*

SOFIA. I don't know what's wrong with me. Don't pay any attention to me.
*Silence, then a sudden plea.*

Sergey, let's leave here.

VOINITZEV. Leave here? Whatever for?

SOFIA. I need to. Let's go abroad. Oh, say you will.

VOINITZEV. Give me one good reason.

SOFIA. Please: don't ask me any questions.

VOINITZEV (*kissing her hand*). Very well. We'll leave as soon as we can. Who is to blame? Mother?

SOFIA. No one is responsible.
*Afraid.*
I'm bored . . . tired . . .

VOINITZEV. Ennui! Boredom! You Russian women . . .
*He kisses her on the cheek.*
Let's be happy. Let's live. You ought to emulate Platonov. Talk to him sometimes. And Mother. And Triletski. Have a chat with them. Don't be such a little snob all the time. When you know them better, you'll like them . . .

## SCENE VII

ANNA PETROVNA (*from her window*). Sergey! Sergey!

VOINITZEV. Yes, Mama.

ANNA PETROVNA. Come here a moment.

VOINITZEV. Coming . . .
            *To* SOFIA.
    I promise you, we'll leave tomorrow.
            *A kiss.*
    Unless you change your mind, of course.
            *He enters the house.*


## SCENE VIII

SOFIA (*after a moment of silence, to herself*). What can I do?
    Dear God, what shall I do?
            PLATONOV *enters.*
PLATONOV. Sofia Egorovna. All alone?

SOFIA. Yes.
            SOFIA *gets up and makes a move to leave.*
PLATONOV. It's stifling here. I shouldn't have done any drink-
    ing tonight. Tell me. Why do you avoid people?

SOFIA. I'm not avoiding anyone.
            *She sits down.*
PLATONOV (*sitting down next to her*). Why are you avoiding
    me? When I come into a room, you go out of it. When
    I step into the garden, you disappear into the house.

SOFIA (*quickly, relieved*). I *am* avoiding you. A little. If I knew it hurt you, I wouldn't have.

PLATONOV (*interrupting*). So you admit it. Why?

SOFIA (*breathlessly*). Don't speak so loudly. I dislike people who raise their voices.

> *Silence.*

When we first met, as students at the university . . . I loved you . . . We were happy together then . . . but university loves, as you told me, Michael, are only temporary . . . you married Sacha . . . I married Sergey.

> *Pause.*

Still here in Voinitzeva . . . and now, you behave as if I owe you something. As if, once in your past, you missed something . . . you want very much now. You follow me around. I'm never free of your gaze. Never a moment's peace. What do you want from me?

PLATONOV. So that's how you feel. I appreciate your honesty.
*He moves away from her.*

SOFIA. Now you're angry. Don't be angry, Michael.

PLATONOV (*returning*). Oh, I understand. You don't hate me. You're afraid.

> *He comes close to her.*

Sofia Egorovna, you're afraid.

SOFIA. Stop it, Platonov! You're . . . I'm not afraid!

PLATONOV (*laughing suddenly after the outburst*). So, you're being pursued. Spied upon. Seduced. Poor pitiful creature, someone wants to steal her from her husband! And that awful Platonov loves her. How grotesque!

SOFIA. You're out of your mind . . .
*He goes away.*

It's terrible . . . I must find him and explain. Michael . . .

## SCENE IX

> SOFIA *goes toward the house looking for* PLATONOV. YAKOV *and* KATYA *cross the stage conversing, just as* OSSIP, *a horse thief, comes toward them.*

YAKOV. The devil only knows what these guests will think of next. Why don't they play cards like civilized people?

OSSIP (*confronting them*). Is Abram Abramovich Vengerovich here?

> YAKOV *and* KATYA *stop dead as they notice his dirty attire.*

KATYA. In the house.

OSSIP. Go and find him. Tell him I'm here.

> KATYA *goes out. Almost immediately,* OSSIP *takes down a lantern, extinguishes it and puts it in his pocket.*

YAKOV (*he is afraid of* OSSIP, *but tries to be brave*). These lanterns have not been put up for your pleasure. You have no right to take them down.

OSSIP. What's that to you, imbecile?

> *He takes* YAKOV's *hat and throws it in the air.*

Well, do something about it. Slap me. You won't? You don't dare?

YAKOV. I won't soil my hands.

OSSIP. Kneel . . . before me.

> *He advances menacingly.*

[28

Do you hear? On your knees. Down.
> YAKOV *kneels.*

YAKOV. You're heaping sins on your soul, Ossip. You'll answer for it one day.


## SCENE X

> VENGEROVICH, *a wealthy Jewish merchant, enters.* YAKOV *takes advantage of his arrival to scramble off.*

YAKOV. Boor!
> *He disappears into the house.*

VENGEROVICH. Who is it?

OSSIP (*insolent*). It is I, Excellency.

VENGEROVICH. What do you want?

OSSIP. You asked for me at the tavern?

VENGEROVICH. This place is hardly suitable . . .

OSSIP. For men of quality like ourselves, Excellency, any place is . . . suitable.

VENGEROVICH. I should have preferred someone else. Not a horse thief.

OSSIP. You didn't ask for a weakling.

VENGEROVICH. Why haven't you been sent to Siberia?

OSSIP. Everyone knows I'm a thief. But no one can prove it. I've never been caught.

VENGEROVICH. Good. You can be trusted. Do you know Platonov?

OSSIP. The schoolteacher?

VENGEROVICH. Yes. The arrogant one. How would you like to . . . humble him? I didn't say kill. Killing is a mortal sin. But just ruffle him up a bit so he can't play the ladies' man. Hm?

> PLATONOV *appears on the terrace.*

Shhh! That's him . . . I will look for you later at the tavern.

> OSSIP *disappears quickly.*
> PLATONOV *stays at the top of the steps.*
> VENGEROVICH *approaches him.*


## SCENE XI

VENGEROVICH. Good evening, dear friend. Are you looking for someone?

PLATONOV. Just avoiding myself.
> *Silence.*

VENGEROVICH. Pleasant, is it not, to drink champagne and walk beneath the trees in the moonlight. Where's your wife?

PLATONOV. She went home. She doesn't like parties.
> *Pause.*

VENGEROVICH (*after a deep sigh*). What a magnificent night. Music, laughter, crickets, fountains. The Garden of Eden with but one missing element.

PLATONOV. Which one is that?

VENGEROVICH. The sweet presence of a woman one desires. Women . . . the sound of their voices in the evening breeze . . . you seem surprised. You think I wouldn't speak this way if I were sober? You don't expect Jews to have . . . ordinary feelings?

PLATONOV. But, of course . . . I . . .

VENGEROVICH. My words seem inappropriate from a man of my position. I don't have a poet's face, do I?

PLATONOV. That, no. But it's hardly necessary.

VENGEROVICH. Well, I'm happy I don't. Few Jews have ever had a poetic face. Why should I be different? Mother nature played a trick on us. We're a race of artists even though we don't look it. People are always judged by their exterior.

PLATONOV. I don't follow you, but I think I agree.

VENGEROVICH. You disarm me, Platonov. You have a poet's face. And you were born too late. Really, you belong to another age. We're all savages here. Half civilized, at best. Animals. Even the widow, Anna Petrovna. Yet, what an adorable creature! Too intelligent, that's a defect in a woman. But what a bosom. What a graceful neck. There, I'm an animal again. Like the rest.

> *He contemplates* PLATONOV.

Why, after all, am I inferior to you? If once in my life I might love a woman like Anna Petrovna . . . Imagine her there between the trees, signaling to me with her long, slender hands. Don't look at me that way! I know I'm foolish. She prefers poets' faces.

PLATONOV. Don't torture yourself.

> *Wishing to change the subject, he comes over to contemplate* VENGEROVICH's *gold watch.*

VENGEROVICH. All personal happiness is selfish.

PLATONOV (*sarcastically*). Of course! And misery is the goal of all virtue. What nonsense you speak! How your gold chain sparkles in the moonlight.

VENGEROVICH. You like these trinkets! Poets appreciate things that sparkle. Take it!
> *With scorn, he almost throws the watch at* PLATONOV.

PLATONOV. It's heavy.

VENGEROVICH. Not with its own weight alone. Gold weighs like iron on the hearts of those who possess it.

PLATONOV. One can get rid of . . . anything.

VENGEROVICH. Can one? You think you know everything?
> *Fanatically.*

How many poor, hungry devils are there in the world? When will the millions of workers ever cease to be hungry? Why don't you answer? Can the poet think of an answer?

PLATONOV. I believe in a better future . . . a new life . . . but for the life of me, I can't think how . . . it will ever come about . . . except for the problems of love, there is no time. . . . Merchants make bad philosophers, and teachers are even worse. I'm going to bed. You depress me.

VENGEROVICH. The same as ever. No one ever takes me seriously . . .
> *A clock strikes in the distance.* VENGEROVICH *looks at his watch, taking it back from* PLATONOV.

Nearly two. If I were wise, I'd go directly home. Late evenings, champagne and insomnia constitute an abnormal existence.
> *He gets up.*

Good night.

PLATONOV (*a thought strikes him*). Abram Vengerovich, would you do me a favor?

VENGEROVICH. What is it?

PLATONOV. Give me the watch. I don't want it for myself. I know a worker, someone who has nothing and who would deserve it.

VENGEROVICH. Sorry, I cannot give away family heirlooms.

PLATONOV (*shouting angrily*). You'll never be a poet. Leave me alone.
　　　*Waves him away.*

VENGEROVICH. Don't speak to me that way.


## SCENE XII

　　　MARIA GREKOVA *comes out of the house and notices* PLATONOV.

GREKOVA. Why are you shouting, dear Platonov? Are you drunk?
　　　VENGEROVICH *goes off.*

PLATONOV. I was only making a point about humanity. Triletski is right. People are no longer generous. If you wish . . . I shall repeat the story.

GREKOVA. No, don't bother. You'd do well to listen to other people's opinion of you. There are things I'd like to say to you myself . . .

PLATONOV. Please do so. It is a beautiful woman's prerogative to be more than beautiful.

GREKOVA. I'm not a beautiful woman. Those who pretend that I'm beautiful are lacking in taste.
>    *Pause.*
Do you really think I'm beautiful? Be frank!

PLATONOV. I'll answer you later. Tell me first what you had on your mind: about me.

GREKOVA. You're either an extraordinary man or a good-for-nothing without any scruples at all. One or the other.
>    PLATONOV *laughs.*
Well, laugh, if you think it's amusing.
>    *And she laughs, too.*

PLATONOV (*still laughing*). You're such a girl.
>    *He puts his arm around her waist.*
So adult and emancipated, not only a scientist but a taste for philosophy as well, and saying such silly things!
>    *He kisses her.*

GREKOVA (*struggling*). But you musn't.
>    *She disengages herself and sits down.*
Why did you kiss me?

PLATONOV. You wanted me to, didn't you?
>    *Kisses her again.*
Look how she trembles.
>    *He kisses her yet again.*

GREKOVA. Do you love me?

PLATONOV (*imitating her*). Do you love me?

GREKOVA (*in tears*). You wouldn't have kissed me that way, if you didn't . . .
>    *Mumbling.*
Do you? Do you?

PLATONOV. Not in the least. But I *like* little fools. When I have nothing better to do. Aha, now she's pale with anger. It becomes her. Her eyes are throwing daggers . . . she's ready to give me a traditional slap in the . . .

GREKOVA. I wouldn't soil my hands.
> *She gets up.*

I told you that you were either a magnificent creature or a worthless idiot. Well you're nothing but a good-for-nothing and I hate you!
> *She goes toward the house.*

I'll get even with you.
> *She meets* NICHOLAS TRILETSKI *on the stairs.*


# SCENE XIII

NICHOLAS TRILETSKI. What a noise!

GREKOVA. Nicholas Ivanovich, if you have the slightest respect for me, or for yourself, you will stop seeing this . . . man!
> *She points to* PLATONOV.

NICHOLAS TRILETSKI (*laughing*). Be charitable, Maria! He's my brother-in-law.

GREKOVA. And a friend, I suppose?

NICHOLAS TRILETSKI. Yes, a friend. Sometimes, my alter ego.

GREKOVA. Well then, I have no respect for you. You see me here, humiliated, and you laugh. Very well, keep your friends. Admire him. Bow down to him, just as everyone else does. Everyone loves Platonov! Except me!
> *She flies into the house.*

NICHOLAS TRILETSKI. There you are! You've been up to something again.

PLATONOV. Innocent.

NICHOLAS TRILETSKI. Why don't you stop tormenting her? Listen, Michael Vassilievich, you're not an unintelligent man. You're too old for this kind of fooling. Can't you leave women alone?

PLATONOV. I'm doing it for her sake. She's nothing but a pretentious little girl . . . masquerading as a scientist. I feel it my duty to remind her what it means to be a woman.

NICHOLAS TRILETSKI. Think of me, torn between the two of you, a colleague and a brother-in-law. Two affiliations. Really, I sympathize with both of you. Almost at the same time.

PLATONOV. You don't need to be impartial. There are moments when you are attracted to the Grekovas of this world, too, I'd wager.

NICHOLAS TRILETSKI. That's none of your business. The general's widow is always telling me I don't have the manners of a gentleman. She always points to you as an example of what a gentleman should be. I think she's making a big mistake.

PLATONOV. Possibly.

NICHOLAS TRILETSKI. You treated that poor girl mercilessly and you say you're a gentleman. Gentlemen don't forget that women in love need their self-respect badly. Oh, I understand you more than you know, Michael. There are moments when we must wound people, wound and humiliate. I know that. And Grekova is always available. Yes,

A COUNTRY SCANDAL

I understand you only too well. Good night! I'm going for a drink.

PLATONOV. Wait, Doctor. You don't understand at all. You don't know what a hell I live in. A hell of vulgarity and disillusionment. Don't you ever hate people who remind you of your youth? Hate them for bringing back the days when you were young and fresh. Everything is so simple when we're young. A strong body, a clear mind, uncompromised honesty, love of ideals, courage, freedom, truth, greatness.

*He laughs.*

But then, aha, we have to contend with everyday life. It strangles us in petty miseries. The years pass, and what does one see? Millions of people with empty heads. And whether we've really lived or not, there's a small consolation; we're surely all of us going to die.

*Silence.*

When you're born you cry because you've entered the madhouse. Don't you think it's terrible? . . . Women are my only escape.

NICHOLAS TRILETSKI (*he has been listening solemnly to* PLATONOV). My prescription to you is . . . not women . . . but drink. Come on, let's have one.

*Pause.*

What's Anna Petrovna doing? Have you seen her? She's laughing and embracing everyone. Just as if she were in love.

PLATONOV. Who could she be in love with here? Herself, perhaps. Don't put too much stock in her laughter. One musn't believe the laughter of a woman who doesn't know how to cry. Our widow would rather blow her brains out than cry. You may read that in her eyes.

NICHOLAS TRILETSKI. You're wrong. Women don't like fire-
arms. Poison is their weapon. Look, are you coming with
me?

PLATONOV. No.

NICHOLAS TRILETSKI. Well then, I'll drink alone.
> As *he enters the house, he comes on the younger*
> GLAGOLAEV.
Pardon me, Your Excellency, here are three rubles for your
discomfort.


## SCENE XIV

GLAGOLAEV JUNIOR (*to* PLATONOV). It's positively indecent to
be that vulgar.

PLATONOV. Why aren't you dancing?

GLAGOLAEV JUNIOR. Dance? Here? And with whom, may I
ask?
> *He sits down next to* PLATONOV.

PLATONOV. Isn't there anyone who attracts you?

GLAGOLAEV JUNIOR. Here? What affectations! They're all
pock-marked and heavily made up. Really, I'd rather eat
than dance. That's what we have to contend with in Russia. You know, I can't bear it here. What a bore! Brr . . .
have you ever been to Paris?

PLATONOV. No.

GLAGOLAEV JUNIOR. Pity. It's not too late, you know. If you
ever do go, let me know. I'll give you a few letters of intro-

duction, a few addresses and you'll have oh so many French girls at your disposal. How's that?

PLATONOV. Thank you. Tell me, is it true that your father intends to pay off Anna Petrovna's mortgages?

GLAGOLAEV JUNIOR (*yawning*). I really wouldn't know. Business doesn't interest me. By the way, have you noticed how *mon père* hovers around the widow? The old booby wants to marry again. As for the widow, charming. Not hard to look at, eh? And what a figure. Lucky fellow!

*He slaps* PLATONOV *on the back.*

Is it true she wears a corset?

PLATONOV. I don't know. I'm never there when she's dressing.

GLAGOLAEV JUNIOR. Well, that's what they say.

PLATONOV. You're an idiot.

GLAGOLAEV JUNIOR. I was only joking. You know, you're a strange man. I can never get through to you.

*Pause.*

Is it true that she likes money and drinks a bit too much . . . him?

PLATONOV. Why don't you ask her yourself?

GLAGOLAEV JUNIOR (*getting up*). I think I will. And I give you my word, Platonov, that she won't be indifferent to me, either. I'll have her.

*He laughs.*

I feel it, here . . .

*He points to his wallet pocket.*

GLAGOLAEV JUNIOR *runs toward the house quickly, and runs right into* ANNA PETROVNA *and* TRILETSKI.

SCENE XV

GLAGOLAEV JUNIOR. Ah!
*Bowing.*
*Mille pardons,* madame.
*He leaves.*

NICHOLAS TRILETSKI (*pointing to* PLATONOV). There he is. As I told you: a wise old philosophical owl stalking his prey.

ANNA PETROVNA (*joking*). Does he bite?

NICHOLAS TRILETSKI. No, no! Once he gets you in his clutches, he lectures to you. Poor boy, I feel sorry for him, but he refuses to get drunk like any Christian.
*He leaves quickly.*

SCENE XVI

ANNA PETROVNA (*going toward* PLATONOV). Why are you so . . . isolated from everyone?

PLATONOV. It's stifling in there. The sky is more pleasant than plaster ceilings.

ANNA PETROVNA (*sitting near him*). Yes. What a beautiful night! Fresh air! The moon is shaped like a Venetian lantern. What a pity it isn't *correct* for women to sleep out-of-doors. When I was a little girl, I once spent a summer night on the veranda.
*Pause.*
You're wearing a new necktie this evening.

[40

PLATONOV. Yes. I bought it yesterday.
*Silence.*

ANNA PETROVNA. You know, I'm in a strange mood tonight. Everything seems to please me. Why are you so quiet, Michael? I came out here just to hear your voice.

PLATONOV (*laughing*). Well, what do you want me to say?

ANNA PETROVNA. Something new and entertaining. I think I love you more than ever tonight.
*They laugh together.*

PLATONOV. And you are very beautiful.

ANNA PETROVNA. We *are* friends, Platonov, aren't we?

PLATONOV. Of course; I feel very close to you, Anna Petrovna. Nothing will ever change my feelings for you.

ANNA PETROVNA. Then we really are good friends.
*Waltz music in background.*

PLATONOV. Yes.

ANNA PETROVNA. Good.

PLATONOV. What lovely music. Shall we dance?
*They dance.*
*Pause.*

ANNA PETROVNA (*as they dance*). Have you ever thought, my dear, that friendship between a man and a woman often leads to love and that the two are intimately connected, just one step away from each other . . .

PLATONOV. That's one step we'll never take.

ANNA PETROVNA. Why not? Aren't we human? Love is enjoyable. Why are you blushing? Tonight your behavior is so . . . strange . . . that I don't know what to say to you.
*They stroll.*

PLATONOV. Do you want me to start?

ANNA PETROVNA. You're going to say something pompous or silly, Platonov. Oh, Michael, you talk too much!

PLATONOV. I can say it quickly. In a word, *why?*
*End of music. They stand facing each other.*

ANNA PETROVNA. Why not?
*Pause.*
If you were free, you wouldn't hesitate to propose marriage to me and I'd be yours.
*Pause.*
Silence means assent, Michael. If you agree, you have no right to keep silent.

PLATONOV. Let's forget this conversation, Anna. Let's not go on with it.

ANNA PETROVNA. I often wonder if you're really so intelligent as everyone says you are. Will you at least tell me why?

PLATONOV. Because I respect you. I don't want to be disrespectful to you. I respect my respect . . . for you. I wouldn't refuse an affair if it were conducted . . . scrupulously. But I couldn't bear to see you compromised by men in any shabby way! I wouldn't wish to disillusion you. To live stupidly together for a month or two, then shamefacedly part company. I don't want any of that.

ANNA PETROVNA. But I was talking about love.

PLATONOV. Well, don't I love you? You're good, intelligent, kind. I'd give my life for you.

ANNA PETROVNA. That's not the kind of love I want.

PLATONOV. Must love always be dragged down to its lowest level?

[42

ANNA PETROVNA (*getting up*). Very well, my dear. Good night. We'll talk again. You're tired.

PLATONOV. Besides, I'm married.
*He kisses her hand.*

ANNA PETROVNA. But you're in love with me. Why speak to me of your wife now?

PLATONOV. I'm a family man, my dear. I wouldn't sell my Sacha for anything. We get on marvelously well together. She's a fool and I'm a failure. Don't be angry. If it were only possible . . .
*He enters the house.*

ANNA PETROVNA. What an impossible man . . .

## SCENE XVII

GLAGOLAEV SENIOR *returns to the garden.*

GLAGOLAEV SENIOR (*suddenly radiant, when he sees her*). Ah, there you are. I've been looking for you.

ANNA PETROVNA. Whatever for?

GLAGOLAEV SENIOR (*a little timidly*). Anna Petrovna, my dear, what . . . have you . . . thought over . . . do you think . . . of my letters?

ANNA PETROVNA. I have received them.

GLAGOLAEV SENIOR (*interpreting this as a go-ahead sign*). I renounce all the rights of a husband, of course. My house is a Paradise and all it needs is its . . . angel.

ANNA PETROVNA (*playfully*). What would I do in Paradise? I'm only human.

GLAGOLAEV SENIOR. How would you know what to do in Paradise when you've never lived there? A beautiful woman . . . like you . . . would be at home . . . anywhere . . . on earth . . . as well . . . as . . .

ANNA PETROVNA. I really don't see that living with you would be that much of an improvement. Pardon me, Porfiry Semeonovich, but your proposal is so sudden. Why should I marry you? Why do you want a friend in skirts? It's none of my business, but if I were your age and had your means, your good sense and honesty, I'd be satisfied. If my heart had any love to give, it would be to my fellow man. "Love thy neighbor," that's the most honorable occupation in life.

GLAGOLAEV SENIOR. You're naughty to make fun of me. I don't care for my neighbors. That takes too much will power. And God didn't give me much. I've tried to do good, but it never succeeds for me. I always end up insulting people. I was made only for one thing: love. Come to me.

ANNA PETROVNA. No. Let's forget it. And believe me, those who refuse are not always the ingrates.
*Noise from the wings.*
What's that? Platonov must be up to something.

## SCENE XVIII

*Enter* GREKOVA *and* NICHOLAS TRILETSKI, *talking at the top of their lungs. They are followed by several guests,* GLAGOLAEV JUNIOR *and* PETRIN.

GREKOVA (*she is crying*). I've never been so humiliated!
*To* TRILETSKI.

[44

Only a man who's lost his virility would stand there and do nothing about it.

NICHOLAS TRILETSKI. Maria Grekova, I beg of you, what could I do? I couldn't hit him, could I?

GREKOVA. You might have hit him over the head with a poker. I'm a woman, but I would not have stood by motionless if someone had treated you so abominably.

NICHOLAS TRILETSKI. Try to be sensible.

GREKOVA (*hysterical*). A coward! That's what you are. Go ahead and eat and drink. That's all you're good for. I never want to see you again. Adieu.

NICHOLAS TRILETSKI. Don't be so tragic. Now she's crying. It makes me dizzy.


## SCENE XIX

TRILETSKI *leaves with a gesture of helplessness.* GREKOVA *falls noisily into a chair and cries.*

GREKOVA. What have I done to deserve such humiliation?

ANNA PETROVNA (*going toward her*). Maria Efimova, really, if I were you, I'd go home.
*Embracing her.*
Don't cry, dear. Women are born to suffer at the hands of men. Nasty things.

GREKOVA (*shouting*). Not me! I'll get my revenge. When I tell them what I think, they'll bar him from the teaching profession. Tomorrow morning, the first thing I'm going to do is to see the director of the national schools!

45]

ANNA PETROVNA. Very well. But calm down now, no more tears. I'll come to see you tomorrow. Whatever did happen?

GREKOVA. He kissed me in front of everybody. Then he pushed me away and I fell back into a tray of caviar. But he won't get away with humiliating me this time.

    GREKOVA *leaves.*

ANNA PETROVNA (*calling loudly*). Yakov!—Yakov! Get the carriage ready for Maria Efimova.


## SCENE XX

ANNA PETROVNA. Oh, Platonov, one of these days you'll go too far . . .

GLAGOLAEV SENIOR. A charming girl. But I'd be tempted to say our teacher hasn't much use for her. It's obvious he's wounded her.

ANNA PETROVNA. Not very seriously. He tortures her tonight, tomorrow he begs pardon. It's always the same.

GLAGOLAEV JUNIOR (*aside*). The old fool. Always following her around.

    *To his father.*

Well, Papa?

GLAGOLAEV SENIOR (*wanting to be alone with* ANNA PETROVNA). Well, what is it?

GLAGOLAEV JUNIOR. Everybody's asking for you, Papa.

GLAGOLAEV SENIOR. Who is everybody?

GLAGOLAEV JUNIOR. At the card table.

GLAGOLAEV SENIOR. All right. I'm going.
> *He gets up.*
> *To* ANNA PETROVNA.

When you understand me, dear lady, you'll know how to answer. Eh?
> *He goes out.*

## SCENE XXI

GLAGOLAEV JUNOR (*sitting down next to* ANNA PETROVNA). The old goat.

ANNA PETROVNA. When you're older, you'll regret your behavior.

GLAGOLAEV JUNIOR. I've gotten rid of him to be alone with you.

ANNA PETROVNA. Ah?

GLAGOLAEV JUNIOR. Your answer, please. Yes or no?

ANNA PETROVNA. To what?

GLAGOLAEV JUNIOR. No cat and mouse with me. You know perfectly well what. Yes or no?

ANNA PETROVNA. I don't understand you.

GLAGOLAEV JUNIOR. I see. Perhaps a little money will clear things up.
> *Taking out his wallet.*

If the answer is yes, you can keep this. And there's more where that came from.

ANNA PETROVNA. Well, you're frank anyway. You don't waste words. Remember, even the cleverest get their faces slapped . . . and for less.

GLAGOLAEV JUNIOR. A slap is always a pleasure when a beautiful woman gives it. First the slap, and then . . .
*He laughs.*

ANNA PETROVNA (*slapping him*). Get out. This instant. Never let me see you here again.

GLAGOLAEV JUNIOR. I won't go.

ANNA PETROVNA. Then I'll have you thrown out.
*She goes toward the house quickly.*

GLAGOLAEV JUNIOR (*running after her*). You're sensitive, aren't you? What did I say to provoke this?


SCENE XXII

*We hear the sound of music and laughter in the calm of the night. Enter* PLATONOV *and* SOFIA.

PLATONOV. I'm out of place in this society. My youth is over. I've finished with everything . . . except sensuality. I'm not twenty any more, Sofia. What hope is there for me? A puppet existence. Growing indifference. A ruined life. And then death . . . If I go to hell, what does it matter? But you? So pure, sincere, bold. How can you belie all that?
*He takes her hand.*
Tell me, for the sake of our future, what made you marry that man?

SOFIA. He's a good man.

PLATONOV. Don't lie.

[48

SOFIA (*avoiding his gaze*). He is my husband and I must ask you . . .

PLATONOV (*cutting her off*). I don't care. Why didn't you choose a man who works? Someone who has suffered a little? Why this pygmy, living a life of debt and idleness in the shadow of a woman who lives the same life of debt and endless idleness? Why him . . . of all the men you know?

SOFIA. Don't raise your voice. We're not alone.

PLATONOV. Let them listen! Forgive me. I love you. I love you more than anything else in the world.
*He caresses her cheek.*
Why do you use powder, Sofia Egorovna? Take it off. If only you could know someone different from your husband, you'd rise above him. If I were stronger and more fortunate, dear Sofia, I'd tear you out of this and I'd teach you how to live.
*There are noises from the house.*
SOFIA *moves away from* PLATONOV.

SOFIA (*covering her face with her hands*). Leave me alone. Go away.
*She runs toward the house.*

PLATONOV (*running after her*). Promise me not to leave tomorrow. We're friends, Sofia. We'll talk again, won't we? Say yes.

SOFIA. Yes.
*Many of the guests appear, led by* VOINITZEV, *a merry crew.*

SCENE XXIII

VOINITZEV. Ah, you're the ones we have been looking for!
>*To* PLATONOV.
We're going to have fireworks by the lake . . .
>*Shouting into the house.*
Yakov!
>*To* SOFIA.
Did you think it over, Sofia?

PLATONOV. She has decided to remain here.

VOINITZEV. Give me your hand, Michael! I knew you'd make her see reason. Let's set off the fireworks.
>*He moves off, continuing to speak.*
Mother, where are you? Come, Platonov!

PLATONOV. The devil take them. I suppose I must go join them.
>*Shouting.*
I'm coming. Don't light them yet, wait for me!
>*He follows the others.* ANNA PETROVNA *comes out of the house.*

ANNA PETROVNA (*she enters*). Wait, Sergey. Other guests are coming.
>*To* SOFIA.
Well, you are pale. You look quite sad. Is there anything wrong?
>*She leaves.* SOFIA *remains.*

PLATONOV'S VOICE. Who's coming with me in the boat?
>*He calls.*
Sofia Egorovna!

SOFIA. Do I dare?

VOICE OF VOINITZEV. Where is Triletski? Triletski!

NICHOLAS TRILETSKI (*running out of the house*). I'm coming, I'm coming.

> TRILETSKI *sees* SOFIA, *stops and stares at her, then leaves.*

VOICE OF PLATONOV. Who's coming into the boat with Michael Platonov?

SOFIA. What shall I do?

> *She shouts.*

I'm coming!

> *She goes out.* PLATONOV *and* VOINITZEV *continue to call.*


# SCENE XXIV

> *Enter the* GLAGOLAEVS, *father and son, coming from the house.*

GLAGOLAEV SENIOR. You're lying, you dirty scoundrel! You lied even when you were a baby. I don't believe you.

GLAGOLAEV JUNIOR. Ask her! Why should I lie? As soon as you left, she began to make advances to me. She squeezed me in her arms, she kissed me. In the beginning, she settled for three thousand. I haggled! Then she came down to a thousand rubles. Give me a thousand rubles.

GLAGOLAEV SENIOR. It's a question of a lady's honor, Kiryl! That's sacred. Shut up!

GLAGOLAEV JUNIOR. On my honor, I swear. Don't you believe me? Give me a thousand rubles and I'll take them to her.

GLAGOLAEV SENIOR. I don't believe you. She was making fun of you, imbecile.

GLAGOLAEV JUNIOR. I told you I put my arms around her. They're all the same. I *know*. And you actually wanted to marry her . . .

GLAGOLAEV SENIOR. Get out of my sight.

GLAGOLAEV JUNIOR. Give me a thousand rubles. I'll give them to her in front of you. You never believe me when I tell you. I know how to get a woman. Give her two thousand and she's yours.

GLAGOLAEV SENIOR (*taking out his wallet*). Here, take it.
*He throws his wallet on the ground.*
*His son picks it up carefully and counts the bills.*
GLAGOLAEV SENIOR *sits down, his head in his hands.*
And I prayed for her, dear Lord!

SOFIA (*enters, breathless*). I'm lost. It's stifling here. He'll either ruin me, or it's the beginning . . . of a new life. I welcome you . . . and bless you . . . dear new life.

VOICE OF VOINITZEV (*calling*). Watch out!
*Fireworks.*

VOICE OF PLATONOV. Sofia!
*Slow curtain on tableau of old* GLAGOLAEV, GLAGO-
LAEV JUNIOR *and* SOFIA.

## CURTAIN

# ACT II

*Later that night. A yard of the schoolhouse which is also* PLATONOV's *house. Included in the panorama are railway lines stretching into the distance.*

## SCENE I

*SACHA is seated at an open window of the school. OSSIP, a rifle slung across his back, stands outside the schoolhouse.*

SACHA. Well then, Ossip, how did you first meet Anna Petrovna?

OSSIP. Well, I'm strolling along the river nearby and suddenly there she is. She's in the water, holding her skirts up, drinking. I stop dead, give her a good look . . . modestly. She makes believe she doesn't notice me. After all, why should she? I'm only a muzhik. I begin to speak. "Your Excellency," I say, quietly, "do you really like this river water?" "Hold your tongue," she says. "Go on about your business." Then she turns away. I am rooted to the spot. "Why are you standing there like an idiot?" she asks. "Haven't you ever seen a woman before?" and she gives me a powerful look in the eye. I don't move. Finally, I have to give some answer. "Your Excellency . . ." And she goes on talking and interrupting me. "Do I please you?" "Oh, Your Excellency, I don't dare say how much . . ." That makes her laugh, so I say, a little bolder now: "The man who is allowed to kiss you is a lucky fellow. Our village beauty, Manka, says I, compared to you is a camel. If I were to kiss you, I'd die on the spot." "Well, try it and see what happens." Slowly, I go toward her, but stop. "Go ahead and kiss me, if you like." I take her by the shoulders . . .

> OSSIP *is carried away by the re-enacting of this moment;* SACHA *is intent on every syllable, the perfect audience.*

I kissed her on the mouth. I shall never forget that day.

SACHA. What did she say after that?

OSSIP. She burst out laughing and told me to drop dead.

SACHA. And you did . . .

OSSIP. No. I just stood there playing with my beard like a fool.

SACHA. Oh, Ossip . . .

OSSIP. "Go," she says then, "go back to your work. Wash yourself more often and don't let your nails grow." Then she goes off. And that's how it started between us.

SACHA. She's a strange person.

> *She gives him a plate full of food.*

There. Sit down and eat.

OSSIP. I can eat standing up.

> *He eats.*

Someday I'll repay your kindness. You wait . . .

SACHA. Good. Then begin right away by doing what I tell you to do. One does not keep one's hat on when one is eating.

*He takes his hat off, dutifully.*

Why don't you ever give a prayer of thanksgiving before you eat, Ossip?

OSSIP. It's been a long time since I did that.

*Silence; he eats.*

As I was saying, since that time, I haven't been the same man. I can't sleep or eat like I used to.

*He eats heartily.*

I see her only. When I shut my eyes, I see her.

*He eats.*

In the beginning, I tried to drown myself; but I swim like a fish. Then I thought of killing her husband, the general, but the old fool died. In his bed. Before I could. After that, I was her slave. I served her. It's very bad for a man to become so tenderhearted . . . but what can I do?

*He eats.*

SACHA. When I fell in love with Michael, I knew he didn't notice me, either. Oh, I was a martyr. I suffered . . . I wished I were dead. And then one day, imagine, Ossip, he came to see me at my father's house and said: "Little girl, would you like to be my wife?" I almost cried with joy. I lost all my dignity and I threw my arms around his neck!

OSSIP. Yes. It's terrible.

*He gives her the empty dish.*

Is there a little cabbage soup left? I'm very hungry.

SACHA *gives him more.*

Thanks. Last year, I caught a cross-eyed rabbit. They are very rare. I gave it to her. She stroked it a bit, and then she

55]

asked me: "Is it true what people say? Are you really a horse thief, Ossip?" "Yes, it's the honest truth," says I. "People don't say things for nothing." And then I tell her the story of my life. She thinks for a while about that.
*Pause.*
Suddenly she gets up, with a strong look in her eye: "It is necessary," she says, "to make a man of you, Ossip! You will go on foot to Kiev, from Kiev to Jerusalem, and then you will come back here a new man and a better one." Well, I went off to Kiev.
*He eats.*
And what do you know, I arrive in Kharkov and meet up with some terrible scoundrels. All my money goes in drink. And I come back here.
*Silence; he keeps on eating.*
Now, she doesn't want to see me any more.
*He stops eating.*

SACHA. Ossip, why don't you go to church more often?

OSSIP. People laugh at me. "He's come to repent," they say. I have an awful feeling when I pass the church.

SACHA. Ossip, why do you scorn poor people? I have seen you strike a man and make him kneel down before you. Why are you so cruel?

OSSIP. Why shouldn't I? You wouldn't understand such things, Sacha Ivanovna. Doesn't Michael Vassilievich hurt people, too? He . . .

SACHA. Oh, never. If he does, it is without wanting to, by mere chance. He is a good man.

OSSIP. Hmmm.

SACHA. In his heart, he loves everyone.

[56

OSSIP. I have never met a woman like you before, Sacha Ivanovna. You are without malice.

SACHA (*as if she hears a noise*). I think my husband is coming.

OSSIP. No, he is not. He wastes his time in the company of
ladies. They run after him, you know. They like his ways.
He's a good talker.
    *He laughs derisively.*
He's always pestering Anna Petrovna, but she's too good for
him. She'll put him in his place one of these days.

SACHA. You talk too much, Ossip. And you'd better be on
your way now.

OSSIP. Platonov should burn candles to the saints that he has
you.

        OSSIP *goes out whistling. After his departure,*
        SACHA *shakes her head, goes into the house and*
        *gets a book.*


## SCENE II

SACHA. How late Misha is!
    *She sits down with her book.*
If only he took care of himself. These late evenings are no
good for him. The doctor told him not to tire himself. But
he won't listen . . .
    *She yawns.*
Where was I?
    *She reads.*
"It is time, at last, once more to proclaim those eternal prin-
ciples of freedom, which had been the guiding stars of our
fathers and which we had betrayed to our own misfortune."

*She turns the pages impatiently.*
What does that mean? Why don't they write so everyone can understand? Someone's coming; Misha!
*She gets up in anticipation.*
Here I am . . . Left, right, left right, march . . .
*A little game the family plays.*

## SCENE III

PLATONOV. No! You're wrong. Right-left, right-left. A drunken man never knows the difference between right . . . and . . . left and right. He only understands forward-back, up and over, haha. . . .

SACHA. Sit down and let me tell you what I think of you. Sit down.

PLATONOV. You are my lord and master.
*Sits down.* SACHA *throws her arms around him. Silence.*
Why aren't you asleep, Sacha?

SACHA. I'm not sleepy. Did you have a nice evening?

PLATONOV. There were fireworks after you left.

SACHA. The baby was crying when I got home.

PLATONOV. Old Glagolaev fainted. We thought he had a stroke.

SACHA (*with compassion*). Oh, my God. Is he all right?

PLATONOV. Your brother examined him.

SACHA. He seemed to be in such good spirits.

PLATONOV. He fell in the garden. That cretin son of his didn't even care.

[58

SACHA. Anna Petrovna and Sofia must really have been frightened.

PLATONOV. Mmmm . . .

SACHA. I admire Sofia Egorovna. There is something so noble and loyal about her! And she is lovely!

PLATONOV. Sacha, I'm so stupid, a boor . . .

SACHA. Why, Misha?

PLATONOV. I did it again . . .
*Hiding his head in his hands.*
The devil in me.

SACHA. What happened, dear?

PLATONOV. It's shameful. Why didn't I foresee the consequences?

SACHA. Come on . . . you're exhausted . . . Let's go to bed.

PLATONOV. Sacha, is there even a spark of sincerity in me?

SACHA. Misha . . .

PLATONOV. How can I ever respect myself again? I can't live without my self-respect. There's nothing in me that anyone could ever respect or love. And yet, you love me, don't you? I don't know why. You have found something in me to love. You do love me?

SACHA. What a question! How could I not love you? You're my husband.

PLATONOV. You love me only because I married you?

SACHA. I don't understand you. You're in a terrible mood.

PLATONOV (*laughing ironically*). Be happy and stay blind.
*He kisses her on the forehead.*

May God preserve you from ever understanding anything.

SACHA. You're speaking nonsense.

PLATONOV (*laughs*). No, really. You should never have been created a woman. What a mockery. You'd do so well as a fly. My dear, sweet Sacha, why weren't you born a fly? With your intelligence you would have been the cleverest fly, the most subtle insect in all the world.
>*He tries to embrace her.*
So fragile . . . you ought to be shown under glass and breed gingerbread babies.

SACHA (*angrily*). What nonsense you speak, Misha! What a pity you didn't choose one of your intelligent lady friends. I never asked you to marry me!

PLATONOV. God preserve us! She is capable of anger!

SACHA. You're drunk. Very well, stay there and talk yourself into a stupor. I'm going to bed.
>*She goes rapidly into the house.*

# SCENE IV

PLATONOV (*alone*). Where would we find permanent wives if there were no Sachas? Am I really drunk? No, I'm accursedly sober.
>*He is about to enter the house when the sound of horses' hoofs interrupts him. He looks toward the sound. Enter* ANNA PETROVNA, *in riding clothes, carrying a riding whip.*

## SCENE V

ANNA PETROVNA. You're not asleep, either. God created winter for sleeping. How can one sleep now?

*Silence.*

What's the matter with you? Have you had too much to drink?

PLATONOV. I'm either sober or drunk. I'm not sure. You're walking about like a somnambulist.

*She laughs.*

*They sit down together.*

ANNA PETROVNA. Yes and no, my dear. You have a strange look in your eyes. You're not afraid of me, are you?

PLATONOV. No. Only of myself.

*Pause.*

Shall we continue to talk nonsense? Isn't this indiscreet?

ANNA PETROVNA. You know what it is . . . incipient old age . . . we're all getting there.

PLATONOV (*pedantically*). Such behavior is unpardonable when one is . . . still young.

*She tries to interrupt him.*

Shh . . . you *are* young. Your life is still ahead of you.

ANNA PETROVNA. But I don't want to have my life ahead of me. I want it now, tonight. Tonight, I feel devilishly young . . . pitilessly young.

*Silence.*

PLATONOV. Why are you looking at me like that?

ANNA PETROVNA (*laughing*). I have stalked you out.

61

PLATONOV. But why me? Of all people. You know I'm weak.
I can't resist. Try to understand me . . .

ANNA PETROVNA (*moves in closer to him*). First pride, then
the game of humiliation. Why are you trying to wiggle
away, Platonov? What good is it? You must give in. There
must be some end to this.

PLATONOV. It can't end when it didn't begin.

ANNA PETROVNA. You and your loathsome reasoning. You
spend your entire life lying to yourself. Misha, if you must
lie, please don't do it on a night like this. Wait till autumn.
Not now! Look at the stars, child! They're shining down
on your lies. Be honest with yourself, as honest as those
about you!
> *She kisses him.*

There's no one in the world I could love as I love you. No
woman in the world could love you as I do. Let's love each
other and hang the rest.
> *She kisses him again.*

PLATONOV. If I could only make you happy.
> *He kisses her.*

You are a beautiful woman. I could never bring you a
moment's happiness. I'd make you miserable . . . as I
have all the beautiful women who have ever thrown them-
selves at me.

ANNA PETROVNA. You really do take yourself too seriously. Do
you think you're really as formidable as you make yourself
out? Don Juan?
> *Laughing.*

How handsome you are in the moonlight. How seductive.

PLATONOV. Thanks.
> *Silence.*

I know myself only too well. These things never turn out right except in plays . . . and even then . . .

ANNA PETROVNA (*takes his arm as she speaks*). What else do you have to say, dear dear philosopher?

PLATONOV. If I were sincere, I would go away from here. But I'm a coward.

ANNA PETROVNA. Misha, you're an idiot. I'm going to lose patience with you. You have only to take me, hold me, put your arm around me . . .
> *Teasing him.*

How silly you are, Misha, like a baby. A woman comes to you, you love her, she loves you, the night is beautiful, what is more simple?

PLATONOV. Anna Petrovna, I love you . . .

ANNA PETROVNA (*abandoned*). Then take me . . . as you would a cigarette, smoke me all the way, and then throw away the butt . . .

PLATONOV. I love you *and* I respect you.

ANNA PETROVNA. Not again!

PLATONOV. I wouldn't permit you to be involved in any tawdry scandal . . .

ANNA PETROVNA (*putting her head on his breast*). Why do you bargain with me and say such insolent things? It's so simple . . . a woman has come to you . . . you love each other . . . the weather is perfect . . .
> *She is saying this like a slow refrain.*

Where does philosophy come into it? Or do you just want to show off?

63]

*Pause.*

Please understand I want peace, nothing more. You don't know, you could never know how difficult my life is and I . . . I want to live. I want to live.

PLATONOV. I think you had better go.

ANNA PETROVNA (*laughing*). I won't leave you. You say all these things in vain, Misha. Look about. Everything is living, moving. We must live, too. Tomorrow we will solve problems, but tonight, we'll live . . .

PLATONOV. Please . . . on my honor . . .

ANNA PETROVNA. Your honor may go to the devil!

> *She throws her handkerchief around his head playfully as she would a halter around her horse. She leads him forward.*

Come, come, come . . . Love me if you love me. And don't be such a fool!

PLATONOV (*laughing*). You're mad. You don't know what you're doing.

ANNA PETROVNA. Come, come, come . . .

> *They embrace.*
> *They hear someone approaching.*

Wait. Someone's coming. Get behind this tree.

> *They hide behind a tree.*

## SCENE VI

NICHOLAS TRILETSKI *enters, drunk.*

NICHOLAS TRILETSKI (*knocking on the window*). Sacha, dear little sister, are you there?

SACHA (*from inside*). Who is it?

NICHOLAS TRILETSKI. It's your brother, Nicholas.
*Sacha appears at the window.*

SACHA. It's late. You ought to be in bed.

NICHOLAS TRILETSKI. I know. That's why I'm here.

SACHA. Why aren't you at home?

NICHOLAS TRILETSKI. Don't ask me so many questions, my dear.
I'm tired. I lost my way. Let me sleep here tonight.

SACHA. Wait till I open the door.

NICHOLAS TRILETSKI. Sacha, please don't tell Michael I'm
here. I'm not in the mood for one of his lectures. I'll sleep
in the classroom.
*He begins to climb in through the window.*

SACHA. My God, I forget to tell you. The grocer's wife is
looking for you. Her husband is ill. You must go to him
immediately.

NICHOLAS TRILETSKI. May God protect him! What can I do?
I'm terribly ill myself. Sacha, let me in!

SACHA. You're not ill. You've had too much to drink.

TRILETSKI. More than likely he has the same trouble. I'm not
going.
*Pause.*
I'm going. A doctor *must* go. I wish I had the free life of a
schoolteacher.
*He exits.* SACHA *shuts the window.*
ANNA PETROVNA *and* PLATONOV *come to center
stage.*

65]

## SCENE VII

PLATONOV. The free life of a schoolteacher . . . ha . . . someone else is coming . . .

ANNA PETROVNA. Don't move.

PLATONOV (*he makes a move to hide*). I'll do what I want . . .

ANNA PETROVNA. It's Petrin and Vengerovich. The whole party is out walking. . . .

## SCENE VIII

*Enter* PETRIN *and* VENGEROVICH, *zigzagging as if drunk. Both wear high hats, one gray, the other black. They have lost their frock coats somewhere and are parading around in shirt sleeves.*

PETRIN. Where's the road? Where are we?
*He laughs.*
Here is the sanctuary of National Education.
*They bow.*
Here is where they teach children to forget God and to cheat. And here lives Plati-platonov, a civilized man. And where could he be now? He must be singing a duet with the widow.
*He sings mockingly.*
Glagolaev, poor bloke/She says no and you have a stroke!

VENGEROVICH. I must go. I have to meet someone at the tavern.

[66

PETRIN. You've drunk too much champagne, you know. Not only that, all the champagne you drank was mine. The widow's dresses are mine. And Sergey's socks are mine. Mine. Mine! Everything belongs to me. They owe me everything. And what have I received in return? They turn their noses up at me, that's what they do.

PLATONOV. I'm sick of this.

ANNA PETROVNA (*holding him back*). Let them go, Michael!

PETRIN (*to* VENGEROVICH). You inspire more respect. For Vengerovich there are smiles and special treatment. And why? Because he lends more money. But I'll claim my share tomorrow morning. I'll ruin her. I'll trample on her.

## SCENE IX

PLATONOV (*approaching them*). And now, you will get out of here.

PETRIN. I beg your pardon.

PLATONOV. You hear me. Out! Away!

PETRIN (*suddenly obsequious*). Why be angry? It helps nothing. Which way are we going? Where is the road? Good night, Platonov . . . Did you hear what I said about the widow?

PLATONOV. Yes, I heard you.

PETRIN. Say nothing, please. I was only joking. I have had a little too much to drink, actually. Isn't that so, Abram?

PLATONOV. Remember, if I ever see you at the Voinitzevs' again, if I ever hear another word about money, I'll throw you out the window. Is that clear?

67]

PETRIN. I understand perfectly . . . young man. Let's go, Abram . . .
> *To* VENGEROVICH.

You're my only friend!
> *He takes his arm.*

VENGEROVICH. Let go of me. I have to meet someone!
> *They exit separate ways.*


## SCENE X

ANNA PETROVNA (*coming out from behind the tree*). Are they gone?

PLATONOV. At last.

ANNA PETROVNA. Those awful men. Thank you, Michael. Let's be on our way, then.

PLATONOV (*hesitating*). Anna . . .
> *Gesture of supplication.*

I'm not sure . . .
> *To himself.*

The devil is pushing me now . . .

ANNA PETROVNA (*hitting him with her riding whip*). Does that feel like the devil? Don't be insolent with me! Now, stay or go . . . as you wish, it's of no consequence to me.
> *She moves away from him, in disgust.*

PLATONOV (*taking her in his arms*). Wait . . . I didn't mean to hurt you . . .
> *He tries to embrace her.*
> *She disengages herself.*

I have the feeling we're making a terrible mistake . . .
> *They embrace, laughing.*

## SCENE XI

SACHA (*appears at the window*). Misha! Misha! Where are you, dear?

PLATONOV (*sotto voce*). You see!

SACHA. There you are. Is there someone with you?

ANNA PETROVNA. Good evening, Sacha Ivanovna.

SACHA. Anna Petrovna! How nice to see you. And all dressed up for riding. How exciting it must be to go riding on a night like this.

ANNA PETROVNA. I was only passing by . . .

SACHA. Michael, are you coming? Come dear, please. And you, too, Anna Petrovna, do come in for a moment. I'll fill the samovar. We'll have a cup of tea together.

ANNA PETROVNA. No thanks. I must be going.
> *To* PLATONOV.
I'll wait for you.

SACHA. Come, Misha.
> *She disappears from the window.*

## SCENE XII

PLATONOV. I forgot all about her. I'll tuck her in and be right with you.

ANNA PETROVNA. Don't be long . . .
> *He enters the house.*

ANNA PETROVNA (*alone*). After all, it's not the first time he's deceived her.

## SCENE XIII

ossip *appears holding up a drunk* VENGEROVICH.

VENGEROVICH. Anna Petrovna!

ANNA PETROVNA (*frightened*). Who's there? Who is it?

VENGEROVICH (*bowing ceremoniously before her and taking her hand*). Anna Petrovna . . . Anna!
*He kisses her hand deliriously.*

ANNA PETROVNA. How are you, Abram Abramovich?
*Trying to free herself.*
You must be mad. Stop that!

VENGEROVICH. Oh, dearest Anna . . .
*He continues to cover her hand with kisses.*

ANNA. Now, that's quite sufficient! You may get up . . . and go!

VENGEROVICH (*moves off by himself, released from* ossip's *grip, confused and drunk, into the night*). How stupid of me. How stupid!

## SCENE XIV

ANNA PETROVNA. Well, Ossip, why are you staring at me?

ossip. Your Excellency, here . . .

[70

ANNA PETROVNA (*taking him by the chin*). Have you been listening?

> *Pause.*

OSSIP. A little. I couldn't help it. The forest carries voices . . .

ANNA PETROVNA (*shrugging her shoulders*). How pale you are . . . are you still in love with me?

OSSIP. Don't torture me!

> *He falls on his knees.*

I have always worshiped you as a saint. If you had ordered me to go through fire, I would have gone through fire . . .

ANNA PETROVNA. Then, why didn't you ever reach Kiev, may I ask?

OSSIP I didn't need to go to Kiev. You were my saint.

ANNA PETROVNA. Enough! Come to my house tomorrow. I'll give you enough money to go to Kiev. Good night. And leave Platonov alone, do you hear?

OSSIP. I shall never forget you like this.

ANNA PETROVNA. Why?

OSSIP. Because for the first time I see you as you really are, a woman, not a saint.

ANNA PETROVNA. Is that so? Listen. When he comes out of the house, shoot off your gun.

OSSIP. At him?

ANNA PETROVNA. No! In the air! It will tell me he is coming. I need reassurance.

OSSIP. As you wish, Anna Petrovna.

ANNA PETROVNA (*she strokes his hair momentarily*). You are a good boy.

OSSIP. But he won't come. He is sleeping with his wife.

ANNA PETROVNA. That's none of your business.
*She goes off angrily.*


## SCENE XV

OSSIP (*beating the ground with his hat and crying*). May the earth swallow him up! She loves only him and I want to tear him to pieces . . . but she won't let me. I must kill him . . .
OSSIP *goes off.*


## SCENE XVI

PLATONOV (*comes out from the house*). To go or not to go.
*He sighs.*
If I go, it's a long story I know too well and it won't end happily. Men try to settle world-shaking matters. My problem is a woman. All my life is mirrored in a woman. Caesar had the Rubicon. I have a woman. An empty-headed woman-chaser, that's what I am. It wouldn't be so pitiful, if I didn't try so hard to get away from it all. And if I weren't so weak . . . weak . . .


## SCENE XVII

SACHA (*at the window*). Misha!

PLATONOV. Yes, Sacha . . .

SACHA (*yawning*). Come in, dear.

PLATONOV. I need a little air. Go to sleep.
*She shuts the window.*

## SCENE XVIII

PLATONOV. Who's there?
*KATYA comes toward the house.*
Does everybody have to come here in the middle of the night?

KATYA. Oh, it's you. You frightened me! My mistress sends you this letter.

PLATONOV (*incredulous*). Who?

KATYA. Sofia Egorovna. I am her maid.

PLATONOV (*dishonestly*). Sofia? Why should she be writing to me?
*He almost tears the paper away from her.*

KATYA. She asks you to come to visit her as soon as it is possible.

PLATONOV (*aside*). That's all I needed!
*Reading.*
"I am finally resolved. I will sacrifice everything for you."
*He does not read the rest, looks up at KATYA, who is staring at him.*
*To KATYA.*
What are you looking at me for?

KATYA. I have eyes. I use them.

PLATONOV. Look elsewhere. This is nothing. It's an invitation to a ball . . . in code.

KATYA. Yes, sir. Of course, sir.

PLATONOV. Well, you may go now.

KATYA. Yes, sir.

> *She leaves.*

PLATONOV. Why does everybody have to come here in the middle of the night? (*reads the letter to himself*) "I am finally resolved . . . I will sacrifice everything . . . Sergey is asleep in the summerhouse. Come immediately. We shall go together to a new life. Sofia."

## SCENE XIX

PLATONOV (*alone*). Sofia . . . a new life, new faces, new décor . . . I'm going.

> *He makes as if to leave, comes back, presses his fingers to his temples.*

No, I'll not go. I cannot go!

> *He starts again.*

Well, let's break everything up, let's destroy everything! I'm going!

> *He leaves.*

## SCENE XX

> OSSIP *reappears and knocks on the window stealthily.*
>
> SACHA *appears in a nightgown at the door carrying a candle.*

SACHA. Who is it?

[74

OSSIP. Oh Sacha Ivanovna! *Call* Michael Vassilievich.

SACHA. He isn't at home. What is it?

OSSIP. God curse them! He went away with her. Aha, if he's not here, it means he's gone away with the general's widow. The widow was here a while ago . . . I heard them . . .

SACHA. You're lying, Ossip.

OSSIP. He's gone. Do you understand? You, poor woman, are alone.
> *He takes his gun in hand.*

Anna Petrovna gave me an order. I will obey her. For the last time . . .
> *He shoots the gun off up in the air.*

If I find him, I'll avenge you, Sacha Ivanovna! I'll tear his heart out.
> SACHA, *livid, stares at him unbelieving.*

Ah! Poor soul! Do not worry about it. I will find him. And revenge will be yours. Ours. I'll cut his throat. Don't worry, Sacha Ivanovna.
> *He goes off. She continues staring, wide-eyed.*

## CURTAIN

# ACT III

*Two weeks later. A room in the schoolhouse.*
*The room is a shambles. Essential furniture: a*
*cupboard, chest of drawers, chairs.* PLATONOV'S
*bed in the form of a divan. There are two en-*
*trances to the room, where they will most strate-*
*gically be needed. There is also a window upstage*
*center.*

## SCENE I

PLATONOV *is sleeping on the divan, his face*
*hidden under an old hat. He is in the state re-*
*flected by the room, disheveled.*
*As the curtain rises, one sees, through the open*
*window, the face of* OSSIP. *He sneaks into the*
*room through the open window. He raises* PLA-
TONOV'S *straw hat to ascertain whether he is sleep-*
*ing. He takes out a length of rope and is about*
*to strangle him when he is interrupted by the*
*arrival of* SOFIA. *A knock is heard at the door.*

## SCENE II

OSSIP *slips into the next room and* SOFIA, *after having knocked twice, hurries into the room in a state of great excitement and agitation.*

SOFIA. Platonov! Michael Vassilievich! Misha, wake up, dear!

> *She removes the hat and places it gently on a chair.*

How can you bear such a filthy hat over your face? Misha, I'm talking to you.

PLATONOV (*half asleep*). Ah!

SOFIA. Wake up!

PLATONOV. Not now . . .

SOFIA. You've been asleep long enough. Get up.

PLATONOV. Who is it?

> *Sitting up.*

Oh, it's you.

SOFIA. Look at the time.

PLATONOV. Hm . . .

> *He lies down again.*

SOFIA. Platonov.

PLATONOV. What do you want?

> PLATONOV *gets up again.*

SOFIA. Do you know what time it is?

PLATONOV (*mimicking her*). You're talking too loud. "I can't bear people who raise their voices."

> *He holds his head.*

77]

SOFIA (*almost in tears*). Look at the time.

PLATONOV (*consulting his watch*). Exactly half past seven.

SOFIA (*petulantly*). Yes, half past seven. Have you forgotten your promise?

PLATONOV. What promise?

SOFIA. You were supposed to meet me at the villa at six o'clock.

PLATONOV (*his head in his hands*). Oh, was I . . .

SOFIA (*sitting down next to him*). Aren't you ashamed? You gave your word of honor.

PLATONOV. If I hadn't fallen asleep, I would have kept it.

SOFIA. You have no conscience. Why are you looking at me that way? I come to you, you reek of wine, and you're rude to me.

PLATONOV (*to himself*). She came! *Vini, vidi* . . .
*He gets up and walks around.*

SOFIA. Are you drunk?

PLATONOV. What is that to you?
SOFIA *cries.*
Oh! Women!

SOFIA. Don't speak to me about women . . . I'm not just any woman . . . Why are you killing me? Where is the happiness of our new life? How is it all going to end? Think it over, Misha, before it's too late. Sit down in this chair and think . . . what are you going to do with me?

PLATONOV. I can't think.
*Pause.*
You think, too. I've taken you away from your family,

your well-being, your future . . . for what? What can I give you? How can I repay your sacrifices? A false and illegal union . . .

SOFIA. Misha, how dare you? Our union is sacred!

PLATONOV. You have it your way. I'll have it mine . . . I've ruined your life. And that's not all; wait till your husband finds out. He'll kill you.

SOFIA. You're afraid of what he'll do to you? Well, he knows everything!

PLATONOV (*freezes*). Hmmm. . . .

SOFIA. I told him everything this afternoon.

PLATONOV. You don't mean it.

SOFIA. How pale you are now. He knows everything, every-thing . . .

PLATONOV. What did you say?

SOFIA. That I had already . . . that I could no longer . . .

PLATONOV (*impatient*). What did he do?

SOFIA. He looked at me as you do now. Terrified.

PLATONOV. What did he say?

SOFIA. He didn't believe me, at first. Then he grew pale, trembled, began to cry, got down on his knees in front of me. His face was as repulsive as yours is now.

PLATONOV. You crazy woman, you've killed him! How can you be so cold?
       *Pause.*
Did you name me?

SOFIA. What else could I do?

PLATONOV. What did he say?

SOFIA. Did you want me to keep it secret all our life together? You seem to think I shouldn't have told. I had to . . . I'm an honest woman.

PLATONOV. Do you know what you've done? You've lost your husband forever.

SOFIA. Of course I have. How could it be otherwise? Why are you speaking to me in this way?

PLATONOV. You've lost your husband . . . forever! It wasn't necessary. It would have been more honest not to say anything. This will kill him. Unhappy man! If we had only waited until he died . . .

SOFIA (*outraged*). Platonov!

PLATONOV. And what will become of you the day we separate?

SOFIA. You want to leave me?

PLATONOV. *You'll* be the first to go . . . You yourself will want to leave me.
>        *Pause.*
Well, it's in your hands now. Do as you like.

SOFIA (*heartened*). We'll leave here tomorrow. I've already written to my mother. We'll go to her.

PLATONOV. I leave it to you.

SOFIA. Oh, Misha! Tomorrow we begin a new life together. Believe me, darling. You'll start a new life. I'll make a worker out of you . . . We'll live on the bread we earn by the sweat of our brows. My mind is fresher than yours. I'll make a human being out of you.

*She leans her head on his breast.*
I'll work too, Misha.

PLATONOV. How?

SOFIA. You'll see! I'll show you what a woman can do when she knows what she wants. Believe me, Misha, I'll light your way.
*For herself, intoxicating herself.*
All my life will be a long expression of gratitude. Come to the cottage at ten. You'll come? Answer me.

PLATONOV. I'll come.

SOFIA. Give me your word of honor.

PLATONOV. I've already given it.

SOFIA. Your word of honor, please, Misha.

PLATONOV. I'll come.

SOFIA. I believe you. I believe you.
*She laughs.*
Say good-by to the past. Here is my hand. Tomorrow, new blood will flow in our veins. Hold me.

PLATONOV. Did you say ten or eleven?

SOFIA. Ten! Come early. Wear a silk shirt. Don't worry about money. I have plenty. Don't be late. Until then.
*She blows a kiss.*


SCENE III

PLATONOV (*alone*). Good-by, village of Voinitzeva. Good-by, everything and everybody. Adieu, Sacha. Adieu, Anna Petrovna. Adieu, Maria Grekova. Adieu, Platonov.

*He opens the wine cupboard.*
Tomorrow I'll be a new man.
*He goes to the table and pours the wine, fills his glass.*
Good-by, schoolhouse.
*He drinks.*
Good-by, children. Tsk. Tsk. I've been drinking. I shouldn't. Anna Petrovna will laugh. Where is her letter?
*Humming, he looks for the letter.*
Tomorrow, a new man. That's interesting.
*He finds the letter.*
"Platonov, you never answer my letters. You are a wretch."
*He laughs to himself.*
"If I don't receive an answer immediately, I'll come to you myself, and then God help you!"
*At that moment a knock at the door.* MARKOV *enters. He coughs to attract attention.* PLATONOV *is so absorbed in the letter and his reverie about it, that he jumps up when* MARKOV *coughs loudly.*

## SCENE IV

MARKOV. For you, sir.
*He holds a piece of paper out to* PLATONOV.
A summons. From Ivan Andreivich Lermontov, justice of the peace.

PLATONOV. Is he inviting me to a baptism? He's as fertile as a grasshopper, the old sinner!
*Reading quickly.*
"Michael Platonov, public insult to Maria Efimova Grekova, daughter of the state councilor . . . damage done to her reputation . . ."

MARKOV. You will please sign this, sir.

>*Proffering a pencil.*
>
>Sign there—received summons on the date of . . . then your name, patronymic, and so on.

PLATONOV. There. And now, will you do something for me . . .

MARKOV. Sir?

PLATONOV. Do you know where Maria Grekova lives?

MARKOV. Yes. Several miles down the river.

PLATONOV (*he writes a quick note*). You will do me the courtesy of taking this letter to her. Don't wait for an answer.

MARKOV. That is all, sir?

PLATONOV (*pours two glasses of wine*). A drink. To Maria Grekova. Her health.

>*They clink glasses.*
>
>*Looking intently at* MARKOV.
>
>You know, my friend, you look like a dead duck.

MARKOV. You should not say such things.

PLATONOV. Then what do you look like, in your own opinion?

MARKOV. I am made in God's image, Excellency. And if it was good enough for God, it should be good enough for you. Good day.

>*Exit ceremoniously.*

PLATONOV (*alone*). Well, Grekova, you're avenged now. For the first time in my life, a woman is punishing me.

>*He falls on the couch.*
>
>Sacha, poor creature, you left without a word. No revenge for you. Taking the child and going home to your father, that could hardly be called revenge.

*Wistfully.*
I was once free as the wind. *Amo, amas, amat, amamus* . . .


## SCENE VI

ANNA PETROVNA *knocks on the door.*

ANNA PETROVNA. Is anyone home?

PLATONOV. Anna!

ANNA PETROVNA. No use hiding! If you don't come out, Platonov, I'll break the door down.

PLATONOV (*looks at himself in the mirror*). I ought to comb my hair.

ANNA PETROVNA (*opens the door and enters*). Good evening, Michael.

PLATONOV (*turning toward the cupboard*). The cupboard won't shut.

ANNA PETROVNA. Are you deaf? I said: Good evening, Michael.

PLATONOV. Oh, it's you, Anna. I didn't see you. I can't get this door shut.
> *He lets the door key fall and leans down to pick it up.*

ANNA PETROVNA. Come here and leave that cursed door alone. Well?

PLATONOV (*unable to look at her*). How have you been?

ANNA PETROVNA. Why don't you look at me?

PLATONOV. I'm too ashamed.

[84

ANNA PETROVNA. Whatever for?

PLATONOV. Everything . . .

ANNA PETROVNA. I see. You've seduced someone again.

PLATONOV. Perhaps.

ANNA PETROVNA. Then it's true! Who is it?

PLATANOV (*fingers to mouth, drunkenly*). Discretion . . .

ANNA PETROVNA. Very well. Sit down.

> *They sit on the divan.*

And now tell me? Why all this mystery? Why be ashamed in front of me? I've known about all your transgressions for some time now.

PLATONOV. I'm not in the mood to be cross-examined today.

ANNA PETROVNA. Very well.
> *Silence.*

Did you receive my letter?

PLATONOV. I did.

ANNA PETROVNA. Then why didn't you come to me?

PLATONOV. I was busy.

ANNA PETROVNA. Why?

PLATONOV. I couldn't. Please don't ask me any more questions!
> *He gets up.*

ANNA PETROVNA. Michael Vassilievich, asnwer me! Sit down!
> *He sits down.*

Why have you not come to see me for the last two weeks?

PLATONOV. I was sick.

85]

ANNA PETROVNA. You're lying.

PLATONOV. Very well, I'm lying.

ANNA PETROVNA. You are lying. You are a sight and this room is a pigsty! You've been drinking.

PLATONOV. Yes.

ANNA PETROVNA. Don't you dare drink any more.

PLATONOV. If you insist . . .

ANNA PETROVNA. Your word of honor. What good is it? Where are you hiding your supply?
>
> PLATONOV *points to the cupboard with the door open.*

Aren't you ashamed, Misha? Where's your will power?
>
> *Examining the cupboard.*

What a mess! What filth! Sacha will give it to you when she returns.
>
> *Pause.*

You *do* want her to return, don't you?

PLATONOV. I want only one thing; don't ask me any more questions. And don't look at me.

ANNA PETROVNA. Which is your bottle of wine?

PLATONOV. They're all mine.

ANNA PETROVNA. This is a bar! You could inebriate an army. It's time your wife returned. I'll send her back to you tonight. Don't think I'm jealous. I'm perfectly willing to share you with her. But someone has to manage you.
>
> *Sniffing an open bottle.*

Very good wine. We'll have a drink before throwing it all out.

PLATONOV *gets glasses.*

You're a poor idiot, but you do have good taste. This is excellent wine. *Santé.*

*She drinks like a professional.*

Just one more, and we'll get rid of it.

PLATONOV. As you wish.

ANNA PETROVNA (*pouring*). Here's luck!

PLATONOV. To both of us.

*Silence; they drink.*

ANNA PETROVNA. Did you miss me?

*She sits down next to him.*

Didn't you miss me at all?

PLATONOV. Every moment.

ANNA PETROVNA. Then why didn't you come?

PLATONOV. I'm going to rack and ruin. My conscience is bothering me. I'm suffering. Ennui, spleen, agony.

ANNA PETROVNA. Ennui, spleen, agony! You sound like the hero of a bad novel. The trouble with you, Platonov, is that you think you're an archangel fallen among mortals. You indulge in the most verbose love-making I have ever known.

PLATONOV. Make fun of me if you like. What can I do?

ANNA PETROVNA. Be a man. That means, don't hide and brood. Above all, don't drink alone. Wash yourself from time to time. And visit me. Be happy with your lot and with yourself.

*She gets up.*

Come to my house.

PLATONOV. No!

ANNA PETROVNA. Get up. You must eat something.

PLATONOV. No!

ANNA PETROVNA. Your hat. Come! One-two, one-two, forward march!
> *Playing the old game to rouse him.*

Misha, dear . . .

PLATONOV (*breaking away from her spell*). I can't come, Anna Petrovna.

ANNA PETROVNA. Well then, take a vacation. Go to Moscow or Saint Petersburg. You'll see new faces, go to the theatre, the opera . . . I'll lend you the money. Give you some letters of introduction to some amusing people. If you like, I'll come along and keep you company. We'd have such a good time, Michael. You'd come back a new man.

PLATONOV. This is the last time we will see each other. Forget foolish, insolent, stubborn Platonov. The earth will swallow him up.

ANNA PETROVNA (*losing her grasp*). Michael, don't answer me back!
> *Pause.*

Well, another drink.
> *She pours.*

PLATONOV. I'll remember you, Anna. Tomorrow, a new life.

ANNA PETROVNA. What has happened to you?

PLATONOV. When you find out, you'll curse me. To say farewell to you is sufficient pain . . . and punishment. You're smiling. Believe me. I'm telling the truth.

ANNA PETROVNA (*after a silence*). Is it money you need? Can I give you any?

PLATONOV. No. Send me your picture. Leave me, Anna.

ANNA PETROVNA. Well, farewell.

> *She extends her hand to be kissed.*

We'll see each other again.

PLATONOV (*he kisses her hand*). We musn't. Leave now.

> PLATONOV *covers his face with* ANNA PETROVNA'S *hands.*

ANNA PETROVNA. Poor little boy. Let go of my hand. A last drink before it's time to part.

> *She pours the wine.*

*Bon voyage!* And all the joys . . .

> *They drink.*

What crime could you possibly have committed? In such a little town, how much mischief could you have done? Shall we have another "for our grief"?

PLATONOV. By all means.

ANNA PETROVNA (*pouring*). Drink up.

> *They drink.*

Ah, the devil take it! I don't like doing things halfway.

> *She continues to pour.*

I'm going to tell you something, Platonov. I've been a secret drinker for some time.

> *Pause.*

Nobody knows it. It's true! I began while the general was still alive. And I'm still at it.

> *Pause.*

There's nothing in the world that's worse than an idle woman. Because she has nothing to do. What good am I? Why am I living? I'm an immoral woman, Platonov.

> *She laughs.*

And that's probably why I love you.

*She strokes his forehead.*

If only I were a professor. Or a diplomat. To play a part . . .

*She drinks.*

It's terrible to be superfluous. Even dogs, cattle and horses play a part . . . They're wanted. Needed. I'm not. I'm superfluous.

*Pause.*

Why don't you say something?

PLATONOV. We're both badly off . . .

ANNA PETROVNA. Stay in Voinitzeva, Michael. If you leave, what will become of me? I want so very much to rest. I need rest, Misha. Speak to me. Will you stay?

PLATONOV. For God's sake don't torment me! Or I'll tell you everything. And if I admit it now, I'll have to kill myself. Anyway, when you've found out, you won't want to see me any more.

*He catches her as she moves past and kisses her.*

Now, for the last time, go and be happy.

ANNA PETROVNA. Very well. Here's my hand. I wish you all the luck!

*They look deep into each other's eyes.*

Adieu! But only for a while. . . .

*She goes out.*


SCENE VII


PLATONOV (*alone*). Gone! A good woman . . . a witch . . . both at the same time.

*There is a noise at the door.*

I knew it. She's back again. She couldn't stay away. Anna!
*He looks up expectantly. Enter* OSSIP, *swaggering.*

## SCENE VIII

OSSIP. How are you, Michael Vassilievich?

PLATONOV (*taken aback*). To what do I owe this honor? Tell me what you have to say . . . and get out.

OSSIP. I'm in no hurry, Your Excellency.

PLATONOV. Why have you come here?

OSSIP. To say good-by to you.

PLATONOV. Are you going somewhere?

OSSIP. Not me, but you . . .

PLATONOV. Yes, it's true. But how did you know? Ossip, you're a devil.

OSSIP. I know everything.
*He laughs.*
I even know where you are going.

PLATONOV. Then you know more than I do. If you will be so kind . . .

OSSIP. You really want to know . . .

PLATONOV. Naturally. I didn't know you played games, Ossip. Well, out with it. Where am I going?

OSSIP. To another world.

PLATONOV (*silence*). Now I understand. Who sent you here?

OSSIP (*sorting a packet of money*). Oh, several people . . .
  Vengerovich first, then young Voinitzev. He gave me all
  this . . .
> *Brandishing the bills at* PLATONOV.

  to cut your throat.

PLATONOV (*gets up*). Get out!

OSSIP (*tearing up the money*). Please sit down, Michael Vassilievich.

PLATONOV. Why are you tearing up the money?

OSSIP. So that you will not be able to tell them in the other
  world that Ossip killed you only for money.
> PLATONOV *paces up and down. Silence.*

  Are you afraid, Michael Vassilievich?
> PLATONOV *does not answer. He seems to with-
> draw into his thoughts.*

OSSIP. Don't you believe me? Go if you want. I'll catch you
  later.
> *He opens the door, playfully.*

  Look, I'm opening the door for you, Michael Vassilievich.

PLATONOV (*comes up to* OSSIP *menacingly*). Why are you
  smiling, imbecile? I'll have you thrown in prison.
> OSSIP *stands at the door, daring him to leave.*

  Assassin!
> *Walks quickly away from the door.*

  Don't make me angry . . . it's bad for me to be angry
  . . . my heart . . .

OSSIP. Slap me, go ahead . . . slap me . . . punish me . . .
  muzhik that I am . . .

PLATONOV (*coming back to him*). That's what I will do.
> *He strikes* OSSIP *hard on the cheek.* OSSIP *does not
> flinch.*

There!

OSSIP. Again.

PLATONOV. You're a repugnant beast. A monster. I'll kill you. There!
> *He hits* OSSIP *again.*

Now get out! Out!

OSSIP (*spurring him on*). Spit on me!

PLATONOV (*retreating, then infuriated, he turns and spits*). There!

OSSIP (*satisfied*). I had a great deal of respect for you, Platonov, once . . . I thought you were a true gentleman. Now, I regret it, but it must be done. I must kill you . . . You don't deserve to live . . .

PLATONOV (*carried away*). Go ahead! Kill me if you want . . . but quickly.

OSSIP (*torturing him*). Why did the young mistress come to you today?

PLATONOV. Kill me. Go ahead. Kill . . .

OSSIP. And why did the general's widow come? Are you mocking her? What right do you have to mock her? Is she your wife? Which woman do you want? Hm? Do you deserve any of them? Do you want to ruin their lives?
> *He knocks* PLATONOV *down and they fall on the ground, struggling and fighting.*

You'll greet General Voinitzev for me when you meet him in the other world.

PLATONOV (*suddenly very frightened*). Let go of me!

OSSIP (*taking his knife from his belt*). Don't move. I'll kill you now.

PLATONOV. Oh, my hand. My hand! You've hurt my hand. Enough!

OSSIP. Save your breath for praying. You'll soon be in the kingdom of heaven.

> *The sound of horses and a carriage.*
>
> OSSIP *stops momentarily to verify the sound.*

PLATONOV. Let go of my wrist! I have a wife and child, Ossip, no! No!

> SACHA *enters followed by the two* GLAGOLAEVS.

## SCENE IX

SACHA (*screams*). Misha! Ossip!

> *To the* GLAGOLAEVS.

Stop them!

> *She runs up to the struggling bodies. All three throw themselves into the melee.*

OSSIP (*bounding up*). You've arrived a little too early, Sacha Ivanovna. He's a fortunate man.

> *He gives her his knife.*

I can't kill him while you're watching. But I'll find him again. No one gets the better of Ossip . . .

> *He jumps out the window.*

PLATONOV. The brute!

> *Outraged.*
>
> *To the* GLAGOLAEVS, *venting his anger on them.*

What do you want?

GLAGOLAEV SENIOR. Excuse us, please, Michael Platonov. We'll stay in the garden until you regain your spirits. Come, Kiryl.

*They go out.*


## SCENE X

SACHA (*on the floor with* PLATONOV). Can you get up? Try.

PLATONOV (*moaning*). The brute!
>    *She guides him over to the divan. He groans.*

SACHA. You're unbearable. Didn't I tell you to watch out for Ossip? Why do you talk to everybody?
>    *He lies stretched out. She comforts him.*
Now stay quiet. Put your head on the pillow.

PLATONOV. Sacha, my treasure. You've come back to me.
>    *He places* SACHA's *hand next to his cheek.*

SACHA. Our little Kolya is ill.

PLATONOV. What now?

SACHA. He has a rash. It may be scarlet fever. He hasn't slept for two nights . . . He won't eat or drink . . .
>    *Crying.*
Oh, Misha . . . I'm so afraid for him. . . .

PLATONOV. What is Triletski doing about it? After all, he's a doctor.

SACHA. He came to see him a few days ago. Just for a moment.

PLATONOV. Well?

SACHA. He only yawned and told me I was stupid to worry.

PLATONOV. You remember what I said. One day he'll die of yawning.

95]

SACHA. What can I do?

PLATONOV. We must hope. God wouldn't take your child away from you, Sacha. Would God make you suffer? Just because you married that good-for-nothing, Platonov. Sacha, take care of our little boy. Preserve him for us. I promise you I'll make a man of him someday. He'll go far. . . . After all, he's a Platonov . . . maybe he ought to change his name . . . as a man, I'm not much, but as a father, you'll see . . .

*Groans.*

Oh, my hand; Sacha, you're crying.

*He embraces her.*

I love you, sweet, dear Sacha. Will you ever forgive me?

SACHA (*after a pause*). Are you still having that affair?

PLATONOV. Affair! What a word!

SACHA. Is it still going on?

PLATONOV. It's not really an affair. It's just a series of misunderstandings. And if it isn't really over now . . . it will be soon.

SACHA. When?

PLATONOV. Oh, very soon. We'll have our old life back again soon, never fear! Enough of this new life . . . it's too exhausting . . .

*Thinking out loud.*

There are too many things in her character I could never really respect or love. Oh, no, Sofia could never be your rival. There are ferments in her which have long since ceased to ferment in me. . . . She's no mate for me.

SACHA *gets up, reeling.*

What is it, dear? Sacha!

SACHA. Not only Anna Petrovna, but Sofia, too.

PLATONOV. Didn't you know?

SACHA. Sofia! Oh, how terrible! It is sinful to be attached to Anna Petrovna, but to steal the wife of another, that's unthinkable! A mortal sin! You have no conscience!
*She goes toward the door.*

PLATONOV. Sacha, you've been reading too many novels. You still have a boy and I'm still your husband. Sacha, stay here! I don't want happiness. I just want you.

SACHA. It's not possible! Oh, my God!
*She cries. Pause.*
I don't know what to do.

PLATONOV (*goes to her*). Please stay, Sacha. I'm a sinner, I know. But you must forgive me.

SACHA. Can you forgive yourself?

PLATONOV (*kissing her on the forehead*). That is a philosophical problem.

SACHA. I'm lost. We can't build the same happiness twice . . . It's finished.

PLATONOV. You feed Ossip, you're good to all the stray cats and dogs in the village, but you don't have pity for your own husband!

SACHA. I can't live with you now. You're no longer worthy of respect.

PLATONOV. I know. I'm a worthless man. But who will ever love you as I love you? Who will understand you as I do? Who will ever embrace you as I do?
*He embraces her.*
And I'm the only person in the world who could bear your cooking! It's true! You always oversalt everything . . .

SACHA. Let me go! My heart is broken and you try to make jokes!

>*She cries.*

PLATONOV (*releases her*). Then go! Go and may God protect you.

>SACHA *cries.*

SACHA. Why did you do this to us? We were so happy, Kolya and I . . .

PLATONOV. Are you still here? I thought you were gone!

>SACHA *bursts into tears and runs off.*

## SCENE XI

PLATONOV. Sacha! Sacha!!

>*He opens the door and collides with the elder* GLAGOLAEV.

## SCENE XII

GLAGOLAEV SENIOR (*enters, leaning on his cane*). Useless to cry out. Madame Platonov is gone. I am sorry to disturb you. I won't be long. Answer me quickly, Michael Platonov, and I'll go.

PLATONOV (*to himself*). I'm drunk. The room is turning.

GLAGOLAEV SENIOR. My question is perhaps a surprising one. And you may think me stupid. But please answer nevertheless. For me it is important to hear your answer. You know her as you know your own heart. You are her friend. You understand her well, Michael Vassilievich. Is Anna

Petrovna to be trusted? Does she deserve to be the wife of a gentleman?

*Pause.*

PLATONOV. Everything is vile, immoral and degrading in this world.

*He falls barely conscious against* GLAGOLAEV, *crying.*

GLAGOLAEV JUNIOR (*entering, peevish*). Am I to stay here keeping guard all day? I'm not in the mood to wait any longer.

GLAGOLAEV SENIOR (*citing* PLATONOV). Everything is vile, immoral and degrading . . . Then Anna Petrovna . . .

GLAGOLAEV JUNIOR (*seeing* PLATONOV, *now fallen on his knees*). What's happened to him?

GLAGOLAEV SENIOR. Disgracefully drunk.

*Silence.*

Kiryl, my mind is made up. We go to Paris tomorrow!

GLAGOLAEV JUNIOR (*laughing*). What do you want of Paris?

GLAGOLAEV SENIOR. I want to behave just as he does.

GLAGOLAEV JUNIOR. In Paris?

GLAGOLAEV SENIOR. Yes, we'll try our luck elsewhere. Enough of this comedy. No more ideals for me. I've finished with this life. Voinitzeva is too small. Let's go, son.

GLAGOLAEV JUNIOR (*laughing*). To Paris!

GLAGOLAEV SENIOR. Yes, if we must sin, let it be in a foreign country!

*They leave.*

## SCENE XIII

PLATONOV (*groaning, drags himself to divan*). Thus begins my new life. I may go out of my mind . . .
>*Noise at door. Enter* VOINITZEV.

PLATONOV (*seeing him*). Is this the epilogue, or is the comedy still in progress?
>*He shuts his eyes.*

VOINITZEV (*approaching* PLATONOV). You're not sleeping. Platonov, you're killing me.
>PLATONOV *sits up.*

You've killed me. Do you know that?
>PLATONOV *gets up, walks over to the wine cupboard, pours a glass and offers it to him.* VOINITZEV *refuses it, turns, then desperately takes it, gulping.*

She was the only thing I ever had, my one treasure. I have nothing now.

PLATONOV. You must go away.

VOINITZEV. I will, but first I've come to ask you . . . to duel with me.

PLATONOV. That is impossible.

VOINITZEV. Think it over.

PLATONOV. Please go away.

VOINITZEV. Give her back to me, Platonov. She belongs to me. She's mine, do you understand?

PLATONOV. Go away! I'll shoot myself! I swear to you . . .

VOINITZEV. No, don't do that . . . God be with you.
>*Makes a helpless gesture and goes out.*

PLATONOV (*pressing his hand to his head*). Why don't I let people alone? I've brought nothing but misfortune to everyone. They all want to kill me.
*Runs to door helplessly and shouts.*
Sacha, come back! Sacha!

## CURTAIN

# ACT IV

*The following day, at the* VOINITZEV *household. The scene is the late general's study. The furniture is antique, the rugs are Persian, the walls exhibit collections of pistols and Caucasian daggers. Stuffed birds contrast with family portraits. In a prominent position on the wall, the portrait of Major General Voinitzev dominates the room. The writing table is submerged under a mass of papers, military relics . . . a weapon makes an appropriate paperweight.*
*It is a somber morning. Rain strikes noisily at the panes and gusts of wind rattle the windows.* SOFIA *paces up and down the study as* KATYA *tends the fire.*

## SCENE I

KATYA. The doors were open. I've never seen such an untidy room. One of our hens crowed like a cock this morning. It's a bad omen. Something terrible has happened to Platonov.

SOFIA. Where did he go?

KATYA. I don't know, madame. He's not in the village. I asked everyone.
> *Pause.*

Forget him, madame. He is a sinner.
> *Pause.*

Think of the master . . . I'm so sorry for the master. He was such a happy boy and now look at what he has become . . . he seems to be out of his wits. It's not right!
> *Pause.*

And you've grown thin these last days. You neither eat nor drink. This new love of yours has brought you no happiness.

SOFIA. Go, Katya, please. Try again. Go back to the school. Perhaps he has returned.

KATYA (*leaving*). I will if you promise to try to sleep.


## SCENE II

VOINITZEV (*outside*). Yes, Mama. I'll lie down. Soon.
> *He enters as* KATYA *leaves, notices* SOFIA.

You here?

SOFIA. I was just going.

VOINITZEV. One moment, Sofia, please.

SOFIA. I'm going to lie down.

VOINITZEV (*he prevents her from leaving*). Lying down and sleeping; that's the only answer my mother and Katya can think of to solve the problems of the world. Sofia . . .

SOFIA (*she disengages herself*). You have something to say to me?

VOINITZEV (*seeing an opportunity to keep her*). Yes.
>*A pause.*
It's been so long since we were together . . . here.

SOFIA. Yes, an eternity.
>*She tries to go.*

VOINITZEV. Are you leaving me?

SOFIA. Yes.

VOINITZEV. Soon?

SOFIA. Today.

VOINITZEV. With him?

SOFIA. Yes.

VOINITZEV. That's the way it is; the misery and despair of one man make for the happiness of another.

SOFIA. You wanted to say something to me?

VOINITZEV. I'm sorry for the things I've said . . . these last few days. I was brutal. Forgive me, please.

SOFIA. I forgive you.
>*She tries to go.*

VOINITZEV (*slightly delirious*). Don't go yet. I still have something to say. Sofia, I'm going out of my mind. I'm not strong enough to withstand this shock. There's a small light of sanity still in me. When it goes out, I'm done for. I know, for example, that I am standing in my study. This study belonged to my father, His Excellency, Major General Voinitzev, Knight of Saint George. A great and proud man. Many have slandered him, of course. They say he was a tyrant, that he flogged his men, humiliated them. But they don't understand what he had to bear.

*He speaks now to the portrait, as if this were natural.*

May I present Sofia Egorovna, my ex-wife?

SOFIA *tries to leave, but he keeps her there.*

No, not yet. You'll hear me out. After all, it's the last . . . time . . .

SOFIA. We have said all there is to say. I know what I've done.

VOINITZEV. You know nothing! Absolutely nothing! Or else you would not look at me this way.

*He falls on his knees and takes her hand in his.*

Sofia, think of what you're doing . . . pity me, don't leave me! Look, I have already forgiven you. I'll make you happy. I can do it. He can give you nothing. You two will go to your ruin. You'll destroy each other. Stay with me. He'll come to visit us. You'll see. We'll forget the past. Never mention it. Please stay. I beg of you. Platonov agrees with me. He doesn't love you! He seduced you because . . .

*He snaps his fingers indicating how easy it was.*

SOFIA. You're all the same, vile . . . where is he?

VOINITZEV (*getting up*). I don't know.

SOFIA. I hate you. Where is Platonov?

VOINITZEV. I gave him money and he promised to go away.

SOFIA. You're lying.

VOINITZEV. I wanted to kill him. To duel him to the death. If he hadn't awakened, I would have killed him on the spot. But he took a thousand rubles to be rid of you . . . No, no . . . Don't believe me! It's a lie. A silly lie. Oh,

Sofia. Forgive me. You see, I'm losing my mind. Stay with me and I'll make you happy. Save me. . . .
>*She is about to go. A last play.*

Are your relations platonic? How far has he gone with you?

SOFIA. I am his wife and mistress. Now, can I go? It's hopeless.

VOINITZEV (*catching at her, crying out*). You're his mistress! You dare say that to me. . . .


# SCENE III

>ANNA PETROVNA *enters.*

SOFIA. Let me go!
>*She finally manages to get out of the room.*


# SCENE IV

ANNA PETROVNA. Have you heard the news, Sergey?

VOINITZEV. Platonov is gone, I know.

ANNA PETROVNA. I was speaking about our property.

VOINITZEV. Hm . . .

ANNA PETROVNA. Yes, that and something else: poor Ossip was killed in a brawl down at the tavern. He never could stop fighting. He made a peasant kneel before him. I knew he should have gone to Kiev.

VOINITZEV (*dazed*). Mother, please . . .

ANNA PETROVNA. You must listen, dear. The estate. What a tricky business! God hath given and He hath taken away. Glagolaev! Who would have thought it?

VOINITZEV. I don't understand. Excuse me, I'm not myself.

ANNA PETROVNA. Porfiry Glagolaev had promised to pay our mortgages.

VOINITZEV. Doesn't he always?

ANNA PETROVNA. Not this time. He's gone, too. His servants say he went to Paris, the old roué. The imbecile must have been angry about something or other . . . what could I have done? If only he had paid the interest, we could have put off the creditors another year. In this world, one must be wary of one's friends as one is of one's enemies. You can't believe anyone these days!
>           *She throws up her hands.*

VOINITZEV. Yes, beware of friends.

ANNA PETROVNA (*concluding*). Well, my feudal lord, what are you going to do now? Where will you go?

VOINITZEV. It's all the same to me.

ANNA PETROVNA. No, it's not. Now, sit down, child . . . first we must get back our equanimity.

VOINITZEV. Don't pay any attention to me, Mama. Console *yourself*, first, then come and console me.

ANNA PETROVNA. The future is what matters. And you have your whole life ahead of you. An honest life of work. Why be sad? You can get a job . . . teaching, if necessary.
>           *He waves her away with a hopeless gesture signi-*
>           *fying anything but that.*
You're an intelligent boy. You're good in philology. You

have solid convictions, good sense. You're an exemplary husband.

VOINITZEV. Mama . . .

ANNA PETROVNA. You have nothing to worry about. You'll go far.

VOINITZEV. But . . .

ANNA PETROVNA. If only you and Sofia didn't squabble so much. What's got into you lately? Tell your mother. What's happening?

VOINITZEV. It's not happening, it's happened! Yesterday, I found out the truth.
    *Pause.*
I have the honor of presenting to you . . . a husband with horns. The loss of an estate is bearable, but to be a cuckold . . . never!

ANNA PETROVNA. Sergey! Don't make stupid jokes. This is serious.

VOINITZEV. Yes, Mother, I accuse . . .

ANNA PETROVNA. You're slandering your poor wife.

VOINITZEV. I swear before almighty God.

ANNA PETROVNA. Here in Voinitzeva? Who?

VOINITZEV. In cursed Voinitzeva.

ANNA PETROVNA. Who the devil could have such a strange whim in our little hamlet? Placing horns on your aristocratic head?

VOINITZEV (*breathless*). Platonov!

ANNA PETROVNA (*repeating mechanically*). Platonov?

VOINITZEV. He's the one.

ANNA PETROVNA (*jumping up*). I will not allow you to speak stupid nonsense. You ought to know where to stop. This is unforgivably indecent, Sergey . . .

VOINITZEV. Ask them! Ask her! Ask him! I didn't want to believe it, but she left me . . .
> *He cries.*
. . . for him.

ANNA PETROVNA. Come now, Sergey, you've made it all up. There's nothing to it. Pure invention. You're such a baby . . . Tell me it's the fruit of your boyish fancy . . . What has Sofia done to cause you to make up such a story?

VOINITZEV (*screams impatiently*). Mama! She's leaving today. For the last two days, she hasn't stopped telling me she's his mistress.

ANNA PETROVNA (*suddenly lost in thought*). I remember . . . I remember. I understand it all now. Shut up, let me recall, shut up, Sergey!

## SCENE V

> *Enter* VENGEROVICH.

VENGEROVICH. Good day to you. I hope you are both well.

ANNA PETROVNA (*to herself, preoccupied*). Yes, yes . . .

VENGEROVICH. It is raining hard.
> *Wiping his brow.*
I am drenched.
> *Seeing neither of them are paying him the slightest attention.*

I hope you are both well.
> *He raises his voice.*

I came to speak to you about the regrettable sale of your property. It's shameful, of course. And it must be hard for you . . . Don't take it badly. It was not I who foreclosed the mortgages. Your creditors were in agreement. . . .

VOINITZEV (*violently ringing the servant's bell*). Where are the servants?

VENGEROVICH. I didn't do it, as I say. They foreclosed in my name, I assure you . . .

VOINITZEV. I'll have the servants flogged. I told them a hundred times not to allow anyone in today.

ANNA PETROVNA. They haven't been paid in months.

VOINITZEV. Brutes! If they had been here in my father's time . . .
> *He throws the bell violently across the room.*

VENGEROVICH (*pursuing his topic*). According to the papers, it is in my name. But in my name also I wish to tell you that you may continue to live here as before. At least until Christmas, if need be. We must make some repairs, but that shouldn't disturb you. And if it does, we can move you into the other wing. They've also told me to tell you that if by any chance you wished to sell your mine shares . . . Anna Petrovna, you understand? The mines your husband left you. You could get a good price, if you entrusted them to me . . .

ANNA PETROVNA. I'll never sell those to anyone! What would you give me for them? A kopeck. Keep your kopeck and choke on it!

VENGEROVICH. They authorized me to let you know that they would take action against you if you refuse to sell. I really must make this clear to you, since I bought up all their shares . . . just yesterday. Friendship brings me here. But friendship is one thing, business another. Such a terrible business, I know.

VOINITZEV. I will not allow my mother's property to fall into the hands of a nobody!

ANNA PETROVNA. I am sorry, Abram Abramovich, but I must ask you to leave us.

VENGEROVICH. Very well. Don't trouble. And you may stay until Christmas.
*He is about to go, then turns nervously.*
There may be a remedy for all this. . . .

ANNA PETROVNA. Really, we have no more time.

VENGEROVICH. My dear lady, if you could . . . would . . . deign . . . to think of me . . . for one moment . . .

ANNA PETROVNA. You?

VENGEROVICH. I hope . . . if you could think of me more kindly . . . as perhaps a friend . . . eventually . . . in good time . . . a husband.

ANNA PETROVNA. Get out! Sergey, kick him!

VENGEROVICH. I'm going.
*He leaves.*

SCENE VI

ANNA PETROVNA (*to* VOINITZEV). So that's why he left.

VOINITZEV (*baffled*). I don't know who's more sought after, you or Platonov.

ANNA PETROVNA. A lot you know, crybaby! You went on whimpering while your wife was snatched from under your very nose.
*Turning on him.*
Neither you nor Platonov is worth anything. Men!

VOINITZEV. She's no longer mine . . . and he's no longer yours . . . Leave me in peace, Mama.

ANNA PETROVNA (*desperately*). Something must be done.

VOINITZEV. But she's his mistress . . .

ANNA PETROVNA. His fool, not his mistress. Maybe it's possible to bring them to their senses. The affair hasn't reached the ultimate stage, I'm sure of that.

VOINITZEV (*jumping up and down like a spoiled child*). It has reached it!

ANNA PETROVNA (*boxing him on the ears*). You don't understand anything.

SCENE VII

*Enter* GREKOVA *in a happy mood.*

GREKOVA. Ah, there you are.
*She holds her hand out to* ANNA PETROVNA.

And how are you, Sergey Pavlovich? I arrive at an inopportune moment, to be sure. Excuse me. I'll stay but a minute. Excuse me, Sergey Pavlovich, I must tell Anna Petrovna a little secret.

> *She takes* ANNA PETROVNA *aside and gives her a letter.*

I received this yesterday.

ANNA PETROVNA. Ah!

GREKOVA. Listen, it's from him.

> *Reading immediately; she can't wait.*

"If I kissed you during the course of the evening, it was because I was angry with the world, uncontrollably. However, you are dear to me, and I embrace you. I behaved like a beast. But have I ever behaved differently to anyone? We will not meet at court. I am going away tomorrow and it's good-by forever. Be happy. Don't forgive me." Find him for me, Anna Petrovna. Where is he?

ANNA PETROVNA. He is gone.

GREKOVA. Michael Vassilievich is going to be transferred. I went directly to the head of the school board. What a mess I've made! Don't listen, Sergey!

> SERGEY *is fascinated by her tale of woe.*

How could I have known he'd write to me in this way? If I had only known! Oh, what I've suffered.

ANNA PETROVNA. Come into the library, my dear. I'll be with you in a moment. I must have a word with Sergey alone.

GREKOVA. In the library? Good. Then you'll send for him. I want to look my fill at him again. Where's the letter? Oh, yes!

> *She hides it in her bosom.*

My dear, come soon!

ANNA PETROVNA (*pushing her gently out of the room*). In a moment.

GREKOVA (*embracing her*). Very well. Don't be impatient with me. You can't imagine how I'm suffering.

## SCENE VIII

ANNA PETROVNA (*to* VOINITZEV). I'm going to see Sofia . . . to speak with her . . . then I'll speak with him. You stay here and lie down. It will do you good. Poor noodle . . .
> ANNA PETROVNA *starts to go out.* VOINITZEV *moans. Enter* PLATONOV, *his arm in a sling.*

## SCENE IX

ANNA PETROVNA (*she notices him*). Michael!
> *He turns to face her.*
Platonov, tell me—is this all true?

PLATONOV. It is.

ANNA PETROVNA. Gigolo!

PLATONOV. You should be more polite.

ANNA PETROVNA. Adulterer!
> *She raises her voice.*
You don't love her, you did it because you were bored!

VOINITZEV. Why have you come here?

ANNA PETROVNA. To mock us. It is unspeakable. We're human beings, too, you ultraclever parasite! Intellectual!

[114

PLATONOV. I see that we do not understand one another, Anna Petrovna.

ANNA PETROVNA. You don't astonish us any more with your high-flown phrases!

PLATONOV. And I thought you were a civilized woman. You're behaving like a peasant. You want me to shoot myself?

ANNA PETROVNA. Like a peasant, I ought to kill you! The way they did Ossip!

PLATONOV (to VOINITZEV, *with emphasis*). Don't forget that I, too, because of you, have suffered . . . certain wounds. I'll never forget last evening . . .

ANNA PETROVNA. What is he talking about, Sergey? Did you see him last evening? Don't torture me. Speak.

VOINITZEV. I cannot.

ANNA PETROVNA. What happened?

VOINITZEV. Have pity on me.

ANNA PETROVNA. Speak, damn you!

VOINITZEV. I sent Ossip to kill him. I hired Ossip. Then I challenged him . . . to a duel . . .

ANNA PETROVNA (*slaps him*). Apologize.
    PLATONOV *sits down on the divan.*

## SCENE X

PLATONOV. My hand hurts. I'm cold. I'm shivering. I think I'm ill . . .

VOINITZEV (*to* PLATONOV). Michael Vassilievich, we must pardon each other. I . . . am sure that you understand my feelings in this matter.
>*Pause.*

I forgive you. I swear it. If I could forget, I would do so. Let us try to live in peace. Both of us.

PLATONOV. Yes!
>*Pause.*

I'm going to pieces . . .
>VOINITZEV *retreats and sits down.*

A blanket . . . it's cold.

ANNA PETROVNA. I'll fetch a servant to take you home. You must leave.

PLATONOV. I cannot . . .

ANNA PETROVNA. You must go . . . Michael . . . I beg of you . . .


## SCENE XI

>*Enter* SOFIA.

SOFIA (*sees* PLATONOV). What are you doing here?

PLATONOV (*sitting up*). Sofia . . .

SOFIA (*after a pause*). Answer me!

PLATONOV. Be good to me, Sofia. There are so many of you and I am all alone.

SOFIA. Michael . . .

PLATONOV. I don't want the new life. I wouldn't even know what to do with the old one . . . I don't want anything any more.

*He waves her away.*

SOFIA. You are a terrible man.
*She is in tears.*

PLATONOV. I know. I've heard it a hundred times.
*Pause.*
Tears are the most superfluous part of suffering. It was to happen and it happened. Nature has set laws and our life has a certain inherent logic. And everything has happened conforming to this inexorable logic.
*Crying out.*
Don't you see I'm ill?

SOFIA (*wringing her hands*). Save me, Platonov, or I'll die. I swear it. I won't survive all this.

VOINITZEV (*approaching* SOFIA). Sofia!

SOFIA (*returning to* ANNA PETROVNA's *side*). I know to whom I owe all this. And you'll regret it.

ANNA PETROVNA. You're wasting your time!

SOFIA. If it weren't for your influence on him, he wouldn't have ruined me . . .
SOFIA *runs hysterically from the room. Noise is heard in the corridor.* TRILETSKI *appears at the door.*


SCENE XII

TRILETSKI (*on the threshold, to* YAKOV). Aren't you going to announce me?

YAKOV. I have instructions from the master.

TRILETSKI. I'll give you instructions . . . on your ears . . .

*He starts when he sees* PLATONOV.

There's the tragedian. Your little story's at its climax, eh? Resting here for the moment, I see. Just a little philosophy before the journey.

TRILETSKI'S *tone with* PLATONOV *is highly ironic.*

PLATONOV. Speak like a human being, Nicholas. What do you mean?

TRILETSKI. You're nothing but a beast, Platonov. What a human drama we have here. Who could have foreseen it?

PLATONOV. What's happened to you?

TRILETSKI. Don't you know? He doesn't know! Oh, it concerns you. But you don't have time to listen . . .

ANNA PETROVNA (*to* TRILETSKI). Nicholas Ivanovich . . .

PLATONOV. Sacha? Is it Sacha?

TRILETSKI (*blurting it out*). She boiled up a pot of phosphorus matches and she drank them.

ANNA PETROVNA. You don't mean . . .

TRILETSKI (*crying out*). She poisoned herself!

*He jumps up and brandishes a letter under* PLATONOV's *nose, shouting.*

Here, read this . . .

PLATONOV (*reading*). "To commit suicide is a mortal sin, I know. But my dear, remember me. I did it because I couldn't bear my life any more. Love our little Kolya as I love him. Watch over my brother. Don't abandon our father. Live according to the Scriptures and may God bless you as I do. The key to the cupboard is in my wool dress. . . ."

*He weeps.*

My treasure!

[118

TRILETSKI. Well, now we're weeping, are we? You've destroyed your wife for nothing, Platonov. For what possible reason could you need a wife? All these people around you: why, they love you, too. They find you interesting and they must be thinking that your gaze is shrouded by a noble sort of suffering. Well, let's go and contemplate the mess caused by this exceptional man . . .

PLATONOV. That's enough . . .

TRILETSKI. Lucky for you I went out early this morning. Except for that, she might be dead.

    *PLATONOV reacts.*

Let's go. I wouldn't want to exchange her for any number of remarkable people like you.

PLATONOV. You mean she's not dead?

TRILETSKI. You'd rather she were?

    *PLATONOV laughs embarrassingly.*

ANNA PETROVNA. I don't understand. Speak clearly, Nicholas. What's the meaning of this letter?

TRILETSKI. It would be posthumous if I hadn't arrived in time. She's not yet out of danger. She's very ill and needs care . . .

PLATONOV. How you frightened me! My God! She's still alive. So you haven't let her die. You're good for something.

    *Kisses TRILETSKI.*

I never believed in doctors before and now I believe even in you.

    *To ANNA PETROVNA.*

Sacha is alive! Let's go to her . . . did she swallow much? How my hand hurts . . . Oh, God, I feel weak . . .

    *He tries to get up, but he falls back on the divan.*

TRILETSKI. Now *you're* ill. Illness may help to purge your conscience. If you don't overdo it, like everything else.

ANNA PETROVNA. Send for another doctor . . .

PLATONOV (*delirious*). Anna Petrovna, help me, I can't see you very well . . . I'm not joking . . .

## SCENE XIII

*Enter* IVAN IVANOVICH TRILETSKI, *in a dressing gown.*

NICHOLAS TRILETSKI. That's all we needed!

IVAN TRILETSKI. My Sacha! Oh, my little Sacha!
*He goes to* PLATONOV.
Oh, dear Misha, I beg of you. In the name of all the saints and angels, go to her! You're a good, wise man, intelligent, noble, honest, generous, obedient. . . . Return to her. Quickly! Tell her that you love her. Abandon your wicked romantic ladies, I implore you!
*He gets down on his knees before* PLATONOV.
Look, I'm on my knees to you. If she dies, my life is over. Misha, my dear, come and tell her you love her, that she's still your wife! To save people, sometimes we must lie. God sees you are a just man, but tell this lie to save her. Be charitable, in the name of Christ.

NICHOLAS TRILETSKI. Father!

IVAN TRILETSKI. I'm an old man. More than eighty years old, you know that?

PLATONOV (*laughing gently*). Come, Colonel, get up. We'll cure your child and we'll drink together yet. Oh, how I want a drink!

IVAN TRILETSKI. Let's go, my friend. Two words from you and her life is saved. No doctor could cure her. It's her soul we must save.

PLATONOV *collapses on the divan.*

NICHOLAS TRILETSKI (*making his father give room*). What are you saying? She's long out of danger. You ought to be ashamed . . . coming here like this . . .

*Points to his attire.*

IVAN TRILETSKI (*to* ANNA PETROVNA). May the wrath of God fall on you, madame. You have committed acts . . . He . . .

*Pointing to* PLATONOV.

. . . is young and inexperienced. While you, Jezebel . . .

NICHOLAS TRILETSKI. Father! Leave the room!

IVAN TRILETSKI. Yes, yes! What did you say? My Sacha is alive? *You* saved her?

*He kisses* TRILETSKI.

Did you hear that? My Sacha is alive! Did you hear, Jezebel? I must go and tell her!

*Quick exit.*

PLATONOV (*trying to rise, a supreme effort*). Yes, let's go.

*Enter* SOFIA.


## SCENE XIV

SOFIA (*to* PLATONOV). Platonov, I beg you . . . save me!

PLATONOV. My mouth is so dry . . .

ANNA PETROVNA. Sofia!

SOFIA (*to* PLATONOV). Are you leaving without me?

PLATONOV. What shall I do?
> *He whimpers and takes his head in his hands.*

SOFIA (*kneeling before him*). Platonov!

ANNA PETROVNA. It's too much, Sofia! Get up.
> *She picks her up and forces her into a chair.*

There's one thing we must never do . . . never lower ourselves . . . never on your knees!

SOFIA (*crying*). Help me! Prevail on him . . . convince
him . . .

ANNA PETROVNA. Enough! Now off to your room and to bed.
> *To* TRILETSKI.

What can we do, Nicholas Ivanovich?

TRILETSKI. Take her upstairs and give her something to
soothe her.

ANNA PETROVNA. I myself should be glad to take chloroform.
> *To* VOINITZEV, *who is crying.*

Sergey, be a man! Don't lose your head. I'm suffering
more than you are, but I'm not showing it. Come, Sofia
. . . what a day . . . Sergey, silence!
> *They take* SOFIA *away.*

VOINITZEV. I'm doing my best.

TRILETSKI. Don't be sad, brother Sergey. You're neither the
first nor the last.
> *Everyone leaves;* PLATONOV *remains.*
> PLATONOV *looks about him at the room.*

## SCENE XV

PLATONOV. I have destroyed innocent, weak people, women.
It would have been different if I had smothered them
under the pressure of irrepressible passions, as the Span-
iards; rather than to torture them stupidly, as a Russian
would.
>      *He covers his face with his hands.*
I'm so ashamed.
>      *Silence.*
I should kill myself.
>      *He takes a revolver out.*
Hamlet was afraid to dream. I'm afraid to live.
>      *He puts the revolver to his temple, quite simply.*
*Finita la commedia.* Christ! Forgive a sinner. Death will
come.
>      *Pause.*
My hand hurts, I haven't the strength . . .
>      *Pause.*
I want to live.
>      *Defeated, he sits down on the divan. Enter*
>      GREKOVA.
Water . . . a drink . . .

## SCENE XVI

PLATONOV. Water . . . where is Triletski?
>      *He finally sees* GREKOVA, *who sidles up to him.*
Well, are we going to court tomorrow?

GREKOVA. Of course not. After your letter, we're no longer enemies.

PLATONOV. I need water . . .

GREKOVA. Whatever for?

PLATONOV. I tried to kill myself.
> *He laughs.*

I didn't quite get to it. Instinct! The mind pursues one goal, nature another.
> *He kisses her hand.*

Do you want to listen to me?

GREKOVA. Yes, yes, yes.

PLATONOV. I'm suffering. Take me with you to your house.

GREKOVA. With pleasure.

PLATONOV. Thank you. A cigarette, a little water and a bed. I don't want much.

GREKOVA. You may live at my house as long as you like.

PLATONOV. And we won't go to court? We'll just go off together?
> GREKOVA *stares at him suspiciously.*

You're adorable. Why are you blushing?

GREKOVA. I'm not.

PLATONOV. I won't touch you. I'll only kiss your sweet little hand.
> *He kisses her hand and draws her to him.*

GREKOVA. What a strange expression you have . . . let go of my hand.

PLATONOV. On the cheek then.
> *He kisses her on the cheek.*

And on the other. I'm delirious . . . I know . . . I love everybody. Human beings have above all else been dear to me. And you, too. I never wanted to hurt anyone . . . and I ruined everything . . . everybody . . .
>*He kisses her hand.*

GREKOVA. I understand. It was Sofia, wasn't it?

PLATONOV. Sofia, Zizi, Mimi, Macha, Vera. They're all there. I love you all. I was at the university and I used to be so kind to the prostitutes on the square near the theatre. My friends went to the theatre . . . I stayed in the square.

GREKOVA. You must calm yourself.

PLATONOV. They all loved me, all of them. Yes! And I humiliated them . . . and yet they all loved me just the same. For example, there was Grekova. I humiliated her. Ah yes, you're Grekova. I'm so sorry.

GREKOVA. Why are you suffering so?

PLATONOV. Platonov, Platonov. The world and Platonov. You love me, don't you? Say yes.

GREKOVA. Yes.

PLATONOV (*embracing her*). They always love me.
>*She puts her head on* PLATONOV's *shoulder.*
>SOFIA *enters, sees them, transfixed.*

## SCENE XVII

>SOFIA *goes to the table and looks for something.*

GREKOVA. Shhh!
>SOFIA *takes a revolver, aims it at* PLATONOV.
>*He sees her and shudders.*

PLATONOV. Sofia!

GREKOVA (*placing herself between the couch and* SOFIA).
What are you doing?
> *She throws herself on* SOFIA.

Help! Quickly!

SOFIA. Let me go!
> SOFIA *pushes* GREKOVA *back and puts the revolver
> against* PLATONOV's *breast.*

PLATONOV. No need . . .
> *He falls down.*
> SOFIA *does not pull the trigger. She lets the gun
> fall, crying.*

SOFIA. Michael! Michael!
> *The others have come in answer to the noise.*

GREKOVA (*to* TRILETSKI, *as he comes to examine* PLATONOV).
I think he's died of fright . . .
> TRILETSKI *examines him.*

GREKOVA. And you were to come home with me . . . mine,
at last. Michael, how terrible . . .

ANNA PETROVNA (*speaking to* PLATONOV's *lifeless body*). Oh,
Platonov . . . I don't believe it. You aren't dead, are you?
Come back . . . one-two . . . now I'm completely
alone . . .

SOFIA (*pushing the others aside and placing her arms pro-
tectively around* PLATONOV). He was mine! He loved *me!*
You loved *me*, didn't you, Misha?

TRILETSKI (*speaking to* ANNA PETROVNA). Poor Don Juan . . .
he wanted a new life . . .
> *To* PLATONOV.

Michael, didn't you realize that love is a dangerous game at best?

> As the curtain comes down, ANNA PETROVNA comforts TRILETSKI.

ANNA PETROVNA. He can't answer back any more. . . .

## CURTAIN